The Magdalene Moment

THE
MAGDALENE
MOMENT

A Vision for a New Christianity

JOANNA
MANNING

RAINCOAST BOOKS

Vancouver

Raincoast Books gratefully acknowledges the ongoing support of the Canada
Council for the Arts, the British Columbia Arts Council and the Government of
Canada through the Book Publishing Industry Development Program (BPIDP).

Edited by Naomi Wittes Reichstein and Meg Taylor
Cover and interior design by Teresa Bubela

Library and Archives Canada Cataloguing in Publication

Manning, Joanna, 1943-
        The Magdalene moment: a vision for a new Christianity / Joanna
Manning.

ISBN 10 1-55192-873-6 (bound)
ISBN 13 978-1-55192-873-9 (bound)

        1. Church renewal.   I. Title.

BV600.3.M35 2006   262'.001'7   C2006-902508-8

Library of Congress Control Number: 2006926515

Raincoast Books   *In the United States:*
9050 Shaughnessy Street   Publishers Group West
Vancouver, British Columbia   1700 Fourth Street
Canada V6P 6E5   Berkeley, California
www.raincoast.com   94710

Raincoast Books is committed to protecting the environment and to the
responsible use of natural resources. We are working with suppliers and printers
to phase out our use of paper produced from ancient forests. This book is printed
with vegetable-based inks on 100% ancient-forest-free paper (40% post-consumer
recycled), processed chlorine- and acid-free. For further information, visit our
website at www.raincoast.com/publishing.

Printed in Canada by Friesens

10 9 8 7 6 5 4 3 2 1

*This book is dedicated to Nick, Kathy, Andrew and Eileen,
my two sons and the wonderful women they have chosen
as partners for life.*

CONTENTS

ACKNOWLEDGEMENTS

I OWE A DEBT of gratitude to Michelle Benjamin, who believed in this book from the beginning, and thanks to Naomi Wittes Reichstein at Raincoast Books. My editor, Meg Taylor, grasped the heart of the message; her skill in refining the text has been invaluable in shepherding the book through to production. Daphne Hart of the Helen Heller Agency has been a constant and wise support. And finally, a big thank you to Helen Kennedy and her book club, and my friends Carole Thompson and Marion Villalobos, who read various drafts of the manuscript and gave me suggestions that were important in shaping the final outcome of the book.

DANCING WITH DANIEL

ONE SATURDAY IN early autumn I came across the prophet Daniel, a magnificent man with long flaming red hair and a beard of truly biblical dimensions. Daniel was selling *The Outreach*, a fundraising newspaper for the homeless. He is a familiar sight in and around Kensington Market, where — sun, rain or snow — he panhandles with a graceful bow of the head and a smile on his rugged, weather-beaten face. Kensington is my neighbourhood in Toronto, and Daniel and I have developed a nodding acquaintance over the years.

On this weekend in September, musicians were playing inside Graffiti's, a local pub. The windows were open to the warmth of the sun, and the sweet sound of a saxophone and bass spilled out into the street. I stopped to greet Daniel as I passed by. He kissed my hand and bowed. I curtsied and, on a sudden impulse, linked arms with him. Before I knew it, we were dancing. Daniel had a Canadian flag in his top pocket, and it fluttered jauntily in the breeze as we circled and sashayed. People stopped to laugh and clap to the beat. A few others pushed through the crowd, annoyed that the serious business of Saturday shopping had been disrupted by such frivolity.

When the musicians took a break, I invited Daniel into Graffiti's for a drink. As we sat at the bar, I learned more of his story. Born in Edinburgh, he had immigrated to Canada as a child in 1950, one of seven siblings. His early life had been marred by his father's alcoholism. His mother, "a strong woman," had left her husband in protest and moved back to Scotland with Daniel and three of the younger children before returning to Canada a year later. He had always dreamed of being a dancer, but his formal education had been interrupted several times. He had made a living by travelling all over North America in search of seasonal work, such as picking fruit. "Good work," he said, nodding his head, "good times."

Now in his late fifties, Daniel lives on welfare plus panhandling. He pays ten dollars for a room with clean sheets at a local bathhouse. Every morning he gets up at seven o'clock and prays in a church and a synagogue in succession. "I should have gone up there many times," he continued, pointing a finger heavenwards, "but someone's looking out for me, and I thank God every day that I'm alive." He likes to eat the occasional meal of goat or rabbit, both of which are available in Kensington. And every Tuesday he gets together with a lady friend of many years. I raised my glass in a toast to life and love.

My dance with Daniel was an act of resistance and hope, an encounter that broke through the quiet desperation of life.

It allowed a zesty concoction of playful imagination and sheer physical exuberance to break into the everyday blandness of society. That sudden eruption of dancing amidst a crowd of staid city shoppers continued to bubble within my consciousness. It brought to mind "erotic justice," a phrase from the writings of the theologian Carter Heyward. Heyward asks us to imagine what would happen if we used the power generated by direct and passionate encounter to fight injustice. By releasing this power into all aspects of our lives, we would see new possibilities and have the energy and focus to act on them. Heyward sees this as our best hope for transforming and healing the world.[1]

Rooted in love, willing to push the boundaries of tradition, and centred on justice — these three facets of the struggle for spiritual change bring to mind the contemporary re-evaluation of one of Christianity's most controversial figures: Mary Magdalene. New discoveries of early writings and a reassessment of the prejudices of past traditions have broken the stereotypes of penitent harlot and fallen woman that have distorted her image for centuries.

The Da Vinci Code, Dan Brown's bestselling novel, and scores of recent nonfiction books on Mary Magdalene have helped to push this research beyond academic circles. We are now beginning to understand the Magdalene's true significance as a close associate of Jesus and a leader in the movement that grew from his teaching. The time has come for Mary Magdalene to be recognized as one of the key founders of Christianity, along with Peter and Paul. Peter's influence has held sway thus far through the Roman Catholic tradition, and Paul's through the Protestant. The recognition of Mary Magdalene's role in the Christian tradition will bring fresh inspiration and creative insights, rejuvenating Catholicism and Protestantism alike, and creating a time of renewal that could transcend the deep-seated divisions within Christianity today.

What if we could allow such a Magdalene moment to open the doors of our imagination, not only to her influence as a historical figure but in a much broader sense? What if we could see the world as the ongoing work of a creative God, a work that is still evolving? An evolution is dynamic and risky: risky because it is inextricably linked with the multiplicity of choices that we fragile and fractious humans deal with every day and at every level of our lives.

Dancing with Daniel reminded me of a passage from Micah that says that God desires no more than for humanity to do justice, love with compassion, and walk humbly with our God.[2] To do justice in all spheres of human life: personal, economic, political and religious. To love with compassion, starting in our personal lives and expanding outward, this love becoming a life-blood that flows through our communities and through them to the earth and all its creatures. To walk in humble partnership with God, however we may perceive and experience the divine through love, which is the essence of God. The universe revolves around a heart of love and justice, calling forth the deepest longings of the human spirit.

In my two previous books, *Is the Pope Catholic?: A Woman Confronts Her Church* and *Take Back the Truth: Confronting*

Papal Power and the Religious Right, I wrote about Roman Catholic and fundamentalist Protestant theology from a critical feminist perspective. Feminism has been a driving force for change on many levels, both personal and societal. My work is part of that movement.

I became a nun in the early 1960s because I wanted to dedicate my life to Christ. Through all the subsequent changes in my life, through my decision to leave the order, move to Canada and teach in the Catholic school system, I have tried to preserve that fundamental orientation in my life. In the past thirty years, though, my dedication to Christ has distanced me from the hierarchy of the Roman Catholic Church. Along with many others in international Christian movements, I have assumed an active role as a critic of the regressive policies that have all but extinguished any hope of internal Church reform.

For me, the time has come to leave the dead to bury their dead — to leave moribund institutions — and to look ahead, to articulate within our turbulent times a vision of the future that is creative and imaginative. In this book, I reflect on the experience of God that has unfolded within the circumstances of my own life as I have tried to steer a course within the unsettled times in which we live. I do not lay claim to any kind of universal truth for my experiences, but share them as an incentive to others to find areas of commonality from which to reflect on the dynamic of this moment.

Religion and spirituality are key elements in the struggle to understand the significance of the human enterprise within an evolving universe. In fact, I believe that spiritual renewal could tip the balance in favour of our common survival. It is my hope that this book will contribute to a momentum for change that is both transformative and liberating, for the earth and all its creatures.

Chapter 1

THE MAGDALENE MOMENT

I AM VISITING the Roman ruins of Aquae Sulis in Bath, England, the site of hot springs that have been revered for thousands of years. Looking over a stone parapet into the pool of turquoise water below, I pause to imagine the pilgrims who have gone before me. As I walk down the curved flight of marble stairs to the pool, I feel drawn into the mysterious heart of this ancient place, sacred to Romans and Celts alike. The steps have been shaped into sloping half-moon crescents by the thousands who walked this path before me in search of the healing waters that bubble up from deep within the earth. I too am a pilgrim, here to experience the mystery. I seek to cross the threshold to a liminal space where personal and planetary histories intermingle.

As I continue down the steps, I glance up and catch sight of the spires of Bath Abbey in the distance. The statues on the façade of the church were defaced by Cromwell's zealots during the seventeenth-century civil war. I feel as though I am treading a path through centuries of spiritual history.

I descend further into this sacred space, pausing in front of a statue of the Roman goddess Sulis Minerva. The helmet that adorns her stone head carries the sign of winged victory on one side and an owl on the other, suggesting wisdom as well as military prowess. The ground beneath my feet was once a Roman brick road used by the merchants who plied their trade in this former marketplace. Under the brick road are traces of an ancient path trod even earlier by the original Celtic inhabitants. The Celts in this region worshipped a female deity known as Sul, whom they revered as a source of wisdom as well as healing. A devotee who came to her pool, here in the shadow of the rolling Mendip Hills, would strip and then wade into the healing waters. Celtic invocations, incised in lead or pewter, attesting to the goddess's power to heal or curse, have been discovered near the pool. A beautiful rendering of rounded breasts carved out of ivory, the offering of a grateful pilgrim, has been unearthed. There is also a perfect cast of bronze breasts, the gift of another woman in thanksgiving for a safe childbirth. I imagine this as a breast-plate from a new mother, who both suckles and shields the lives entrusted to her care.

Close by the statues and other offerings, I pause to dip my hands in the turquoise pool and splash my face with the warm water. The pool is cloudy yet luminescent. Heat rises from the surface. A little girl beside me unclasps the buckle on her tiny sandal to dip her foot gingerly into the water.

I wonder what the future holds for her.

Resting on the low stone wall surrounding the pool, I contemplate the origins of the water flowing through my hands. The spring that bubbles up here began as drops of rain that fell ten thousand years ago on the nearby Mendip Hills. Over thousands of years the water seeped down through layers of carboniferous limestone. There, deep within the earth, blistering heat transformed the water into steam, which pushes upwards, refreshing and cleansing the earth's surface.

I sit still, listening to the spring water flowing beside the pool. More than one million litres a day flow out of the goddess's spring and into the pool; more than a litre per second drains into the nearby River Avon.

The epic journey of these waters testifies to the primordial connection that links air, earth, fire and rock. From the skies above to the fires beneath the earth and the waters on the surface, everything is connected to the very pulse of the planet. The ten-thousand-year history of the waters of Bath is but a small blip in the history of the world. But unless we act soon to change our ways, we humans are on the brink of disrupting the natural cycles that have sustained and nourished all life on the planet.

Ten thousand years ago, when drops of rain fell from the sky there was no chemical sludge on the ground, polluting the rainwater as it sought an opening in the earth's surface to penetrate to the rock beneath and so pass into the furnace of heat below. Our ancestors would have paused to gather up some of the pristine rainfall to slake their thirst with no concern about its chemical content. Thus this water would enter into the evolving body of humankind, passed on to future generations through the genetic inheritance that links us to the earliest forerunners of our species.

Sul's name, so close to the Latin word *sol*, suggests to me that she might have been connected to the sun. The sun was revered by many early peoples as a symbol of feminine warmth that made the earth and its crops fertile and gave life to the universe. In Aztec, Celtic and Roman cultures, women were the keepers of the flame. Here, the stream of water warmed at the heart of the earth finds a path to the surface through the thin fissures in the petrified layers of rock, providing healing in a place known for its life-giving properties.

I am reminded of the thin fissures in the petrified layers of religion today, where a new understanding of the relationship between God, creation and humanity is filtering through as new streams of spirituality arise within the consciousness of so many seekers. To uncover again the sacredness of creation — the holiness of water, sun and earth — and accord them due honour as living components of God's revelation is one of the most urgent tasks of the present moment in history.

My journey to Bath was something of a homecoming for me, a return to my birthplace and that of my ancestors in England. Likewise, it seems that the whole human race is now entering a period of homecoming after a long exile from the earth. The dualism that has haunted Christianity since it adopted from Greek philosophy the idea of a split between soul and body has exiled us from our roots by teaching us to look to heaven in search of a distant God rather than to feel the pulse of God's heart within the rhythm of the earth beneath our feet. The transcendent God of patriarchal religion is distant, exalted in a heaven beyond the clouds.

Living in modern industrial and post-industrial societies, we are cut off from our origins and forget that our roots lie deep within the earth. We have been alienated from these roots and cut off from the sacredness of earth's waters and forests. Religion has suppressed the sacred feminine, and dishonoured the healing power of the sensual world. As we come to realize the connections between the fate of the earth and the way we live out our economic, political, and religious existence, our eyes have been opened to the nearness of God, the immanent source of all life within the cosmos and the sacred creative presence that powers the universe. Human consciousness is changing as we become more aware of global warming, species extinction, inequities between rich and poor and the ravages of runaway consumption in the richest societies. An emerging awareness that celebrates unity and common ground is increasingly compelling. It is, however, under threat from the re-emergence of fundamentalism in so many parts of the globe. To change this will require an evolution in the human understanding of God, the relationship of God with humanity and the interdependence of humanity and creation. At the outset of this twenty-first century, it is unspeakably sad to see God's name invoked over and over again as a sanction for large-scale violence, oppression, hatred and murder. The intractability of institutionalized religions and global politics is propelling us along a pathway that may plunge us into a new dark age of mutually assured destruction. Environmental pollution and global warming threaten many species, including our own. Wars engulf many parts of the world, draining economic resources and political energy. The chasm between the rich and the poor is widening. Abuse and violence against women are still prevalent. The fragile balance of the ecosystem is threatened by our inability to work together to ensure a future for our children. We must break down the old boundaries of religion, gender and ethnicity to put an end to oppression and violence. Only then will we be able to join together to save the planet. This has become the most urgent task facing humanity today. And no God is going to descend from the sky to rescue us.

In the United States, evangelical Christians now control the right wing of the Republican Party, having found new allies among Catholic conservatives. At the United Nations, this alliance has led to support from the U.S. for the Vatican's continuing campaign against women's equality and reproductive rights: an about-face from the Clinton era, when the U.S. delegation was not beholden to the Religious Right. Catholic papal fundamentalists, who believe in a rigidly hierarchical church and unquestioning obedience to the Pope, and Protestant biblical fundamentalists, who extrapolate certain passages from the Bible and interpret them literally, without any heed to their context, have discovered common ground over issues such as abortion, gay rights, abstinence-only sex education, Christian exclusivism, "family values," free-market capitalism, and contempt for the struggle to save the environment.

At the most extreme end of evangelical Protestantism are those who believe in the Rapture. According to them, when Christ returns to "judge the quick and the dead," the followers of the true faith, including those who will arise from their graves, will ascend into eternal salvation in heaven. Everyone else will then be destroyed in the battle of Armageddon. Why, then, should they care about scientific prognostications of an eventual environmental catastrophe, if the whole world will go up in flames soon anyway? Why not open up the Alaskan wilderness to drilling for oil, since the whole of the Arctic will soon be blasted out of existence by the flaming breath of God's wrath?

The Rapture is the most nihilistic version of the dualistic spirituality that has alienated humanity from the earth. Belief in the Rapture absolves its adherents from taking action to ameliorate the here and now, because they believe the earth is transitory and corrupted by sin. Furthermore, they believe that the poor are poor because they have not found favour with God, who rewards his followers with wealth and prosperity. Ever since Adam and Eve fell into sexual sin, according to their tenets, a violent and vengeful God has sought ways to punish humanity and destroy the earth. And despite modern discoveries of the nature and extent of the universe, and the interconnectedness of all life forms, Christian worship in general remains locked into symbolism and forms of prayer that emphasize the separation between earth and heaven.

Right-wing Catholics don't believe in the Rapture, but during the papacy of the late John Paul II, Catholic spirituality also made an about-turn. When the former Cardinal Josef Ratzinger was elected as Pope Benedict XVI in 2005, I lost all remaining hope that the Catholic Church would be reformed from within, as many had hoped after the Second Vatican Council (1962–65). Catholics don't believe that priests and clergy are destined to be directly raptured into heaven in the Last Days, but the reassertion of hierarchical control within the Church has catapulted the clergy right back to the top of the heap of humanity here on earth. There has also been a return to the stifling culture of unquestioning reverence for the person of the Pope, which hearkens back to when I was growing up Catholic in the 1950s. The idolatry of the papal office that was displayed at the funeral of John Paul II, and magnified a thousand-fold by the media, has been accompanied by a return to sharp hierarchical divisions between laity and priests, and women and men — something that Pope John Paul II adopted as a personal crusade in his declining years. Together with the systematic crushing of internal questioning and dissent, this has served to eliminate the hope of reform awakened in the 1960s by the Second Vatican Council.

And so I often ask myself: does this re-emergence of male-dominated hegemony in Protestant and Catholic Christianity mean that feminist and pluralistic rethinking of Christian theology has been just a flash on a radar screen that is now flickering on the verge of a shutdown? It could very well be. I do not pretend to have a privileged eye into the future, and the coming years could belong to the conservative Christians in all denominations, backed as they are by the superior firepower of the United States.

Much of institutionalized religion has now become toxic to the future survival of the earth. Religion is not the only toxic force in the world today, but it is among the most powerful. We may have entered into a very dark period of history indeed, with the world divided not only along religious fault lines but also between the haves and the have-nots within each nation. Humanity has just entered the twenty-first century, but the institutional forces of conservative religion seem to be intent on assuring that this will be its last.

The precepts of the Religious Right, Catholic as well as Protestant, run counter to my experience of God. I celebrate the fact that humanity is beginning to cast off the false patriarchal religiosity that has distanced us from the sacred. For centuries we have been told to look for God outside ourselves, whether in the literal interpretation of sacred texts such as the Bible, or through an ecclesiastical power structure of priests and ministers, or via the spiritual infallibility of the Catholic papacy. One by one, and again and again, these have fallen short and failed to nourish the contemporary hunger for the sacred. But as religious institutions falter, God is breaking out of captivity. God's spirit is now at work forcing us to rethink our place in this vast universe, to honour the wonder of its diversity and perpetual motion, and to embrace it with awe and graciousness instead of trying to exploit it, motivated only by fear and greed.

God is near. Not the patriarchal, violent, exclusive God of the past, but a compassionate and all-embracing God of the future. A modern religious reformation has begun, a breakthrough into a new spiritual consciousness that cuts across denominational and religious boundaries. This is why the current rediscovery and re-evaluation of Mary Magdalene is, for me, such an important sign of hope. New life is springing from the fertile earth of the ancient Magdalene tradition, now watered and enriched by modern justice movements — anti-poverty, anti-war, and environmental. This mingling of the ancient Magdalene tradition with the modern search for spiritual meaning and social justice is what I am calling the Magdalene moment.

We now know that Mary Magdalene played a pivotal role in the origin and development of Christianity. She was the primary witness to the resurrection of Jesus. Had she and the other women not held to their conviction that Jesus was alive, the other followers would have remained locked in fear in the upper room. So Mary Magdalene was the primary architect of the Easter faith, the apostle to the apostles, to whom Jesus entrusted his most vital message: that the movement he initiated had not died with his crucifixion but had burst forth from the sepulchre and into a higher dimension of existence.

The reinstatement of the Magdalene as a central figure in the life of Jesus and the early Christian church has been occurring in academic books and articles for more than thirty years. Recently, popular literature has exposed a much wider audience to this new understanding of Mary of Magdala's role as the chosen companion, maybe even successor, to Jesus, and the possibilities this holds for the future evolution of Christianity. The discovery of a rich cache of Gnostic Christian texts in Egypt in 1945 lends credence to the idea that women held positions of leadership at the inception of Christianity. The unearthed manuscripts brought to light several accounts of the life and teachings of Jesus, and other sacred texts that had been suppressed by the early church. The thirteen leather-bound papyrus codices containing more than fifty texts were uncovered quite accidentally by a peasant who was digging in the hills near the town of Nag Hammadi in central Egypt. Translations were completed in the 1970s and led to a major re-evaluation of early Christian history.

The synchronicity of this discovery with the beginnings of theological and scriptural studies by women has been exhilarating. This scholarship demonstrates the leadership role of Mary Magdalene in the early church and supports efforts to open up the structures of modern Christian communities to mutual partnerships between men and women at all levels. In *The Resurrection of Mary Magdalene*, the religious scholar Jane Schaberg introduces the notion that the time is propitious for a Magdalene Christianity.[1] She contends that the Petrine model of Christianity, identified as the Roman Catholic Church, and the Pauline model, identified as the Protestant tradition, are both in serious trouble. Magdalene Christianity would re-establish the prophetic leadership of women that was suppressed early in Christian history and would acknowledge that Mary Magdalene, as much as Peter or Paul, played a crucial role in transmitting the message of Jesus and inaugurating the church. Schaberg calls her "a creator of the Easter faith."[2]

It is hard for us now to imagine a Christian setting without the New Testament, the Nicene Creed and the Apostles' Creed, and no established church hierarchy or chain of command. But current church structures and rules are a product of the Roman imperial framework in which they arose rather than of any direct instruction from Jesus. In its first two centuries, Christianity harboured a diversity of voices and movements. Jesus himself is a stunning role model for the articulation of an alternative consciousness within the religious institutions of his day. Other discoveries of previously unknown writing from early Christian sources, such as the Gospel of Mary and the Gospel of Thomas, attest to the vibrant and pluralistic nature of the Christian world in the first two centuries after the death of Jesus.

The manuscript of the Gospel of Mary came to light in an antique market in Cairo in 1896. This and several of the very early writings that were brought to light again only in the mid-twentieth century demonstrate the central position of Mary Magdalene and provide convincing evidence of women's leadership role in the beginnings of Christianity. The *Dialogue of the Saviour*, a Nag Hammadi discovery dating from the early second century, names Mary as one of the three apostles that Jesus made leaders. In the *Sophia of Christ*, from the same era, she is listed as part of an inner group of five, the others being Matthew, Thomas, Philip and Bartholomew: a different group from the more traditional one of Peter, Andrew, James and John.

In the Gospel of Mary, the Magdalene gives the other apostles a special teaching that Jesus gave to her alone, and she comforts the distraught group of disciples after Jesus has departed. Peter at first defers to her superior knowledge of Jesus. "Sister," he says, "we know that the Saviour loved you more than any other woman. Tell us the words of the Saviour that you know, but which we haven't heard."[3] But after she has spoken, first Andrew and then Peter begin to question her authority. "Has the Saviour spoken secretly to a woman?" Peter exclaimed, "and not openly so that we would all hear? Surely he did not wish to indicate that she is more worthy than we are?"[4]

After this verbal attack, Mary weeps. Levi rallies to her defence: "Peter, you have a constant inclination to anger and you are always ready to give way to it. And even now you are doing exactly that by questioning the woman as if you are her adversary. If the Saviour considered her to be worthy, who are you to disregard her? For he knew her completely and loved her devotedly."[5] "The Gospel of Mary," writes Professor Antti Marjanen, "affirms the legitimacy of women's leadership role," a role that is "not based simply on being one of the Twelve or on gender but on spiritual qualifications."[6]

In the Gospel of Thomas, Peter attempts to have Mary Magdalene expelled from the group of disciples. "Let Mary leave us," he says to Jesus, "because women are not worthy of life."[7]

How fascinating that these words have been echoed from the papal office so often in recent years as the controversy over women's equality in the company of disciples continues to preoccupy Catholic leaders.

In this account, Jesus refuses to acquiesce to Peter's request. "Look," he says to Peter, "I myself will lead her," adding, "so that I will make her male in order that she too may become a living spirit, resembling you males. For every woman who makes herself male will enter the kingdom of heaven."[8] Needless to say, Jesus' enigmatic and, at least on the surface, denigrating remark about "making her male" has stirred up considerable controversy. It could be an allusion to the androgynous nature of the first human, Adam, before he and Eve became separate parts of the first human entity in the creation story as it is told in the second chapter of Genesis.[9] It may also be an affirmation of the ascetic practices favoured by some adherents of Gnosticism, which highly valued celibacy. It could mean too that Jesus intended Mary to be accepted by the male disciples as a full equal, not confined by societal restrictions on her gender.

When I first came across the "making her male" phrase from the Gospel of Thomas, it reminded me of the struggles that women entering the work force in the twentieth century underwent in order to prove that they were as capable as men. In the 1980s I was principal of a high school in Toronto, and in that capacity I attended the meetings held every month between the superintendent of education and the local high school principals. I was the only woman in the group.

Once, when the superintendent referred to all of us as "you fellows," I remarked that we were not all included in that term. "But Joanna," he responded, "I always think of you as a man — and that's intended as a compliment." So I too had undergone a similar process within that group, of "being made a male" in order to be treated as an equal.

Early evidence of the rivalry between Peter and Mary Magdalene, "the most polemically charged figures in Christian history," according to Ann Graham Brock of Harvard Divinity School, may very well indicate that the nature and role of women was a hotly disputed issue in early Christian communities.[10] Hippolytus, the early third-century bishop of Rome, wrote: "Lest the female apostles doubt the angels, Christ himself came to them so that the women would be apostles of Christ ... Christ showed himself to the apostles and said to them ... 'It is I who appeared to these women and I who wanted to send them to you as apostles.'"[11]

The farther one goes back toward the source, to Jesus himself, the greater is the evidence for the leading role Mary Magdalene played within the group of apostles. In three of the four canonical gospels (Luke being the exception) she is the most consistent witness to the resurrection of Jesus. In each of the four gospels she is directed to go and tell the other disciples what she has seen and heard. Her vital importance in the creation of early Christian communities is reflected in the Gnostic gospels, the sacred texts rediscovered in modern times. But as Roman culture began to dominate society, the imperial structure was gradually adopted by the church, and Mary Magdalene was censored out of the tradition.

As the early Christian communities spread within the Roman Empire, the leadership of women and their capacity to act in partnership with men declined under the influence of the Roman family structure, which emphasized the role of the man as paterfamilias and head of household. An early example of the deliberate suppression of Mary Magdalene's leadership comes from evidence that in some communities, Mary the mother of Jesus had usurped the Magdalene's role in the resurrection. The text of the later Greek *Acta Thaddaei* reads as follows: "He [Jesus] appeared first to his mother and to the other women, and to Peter and John, the first of my co-disciples and then also to us the twelve who ate and drank with him after his resurrection."[12] It is interesting that this text, which makes no mention of Mary Magdalene by name, also emphasizes the role of Peter along with John as the first among the disciples. Mary, Jesus' mother, is also portrayed as bolstering the prominence of Peter.

Several Syriac and Coptic texts also substitute Jesus' mother for Mary Magdalene. Brock argues that this represents a deliberate attempt to diminish the role of the Magdalene as both the closest companion of Jesus and his chosen first witness to the resurrection. Texts that honour Mary the Mother also highlight the role of Peter. How remarkable that these discoveries should have come to light in an era when Peter's successors, the popes of the twentieth and twenty-first centuries, have exalted Mary the mother of Jesus as a role model for contemporary women: a deliberate strategy on the part of

popes ancient and modern to prevent women from identify-
ing either with Christ himself or with the more assertive
Mary Magdalene.

The predominant female role model within Christianity,
especially the Roman Catholic variety, has hitherto been Mary,
the mother of Jesus. The church has succeeded in swaddling
the sexuality of Mary within the boundaries of virginity and
procreation. Under the custodianship of celibate men, Mary's
life has been carefully shielded within the confines of perpetual chastity. There was once a time when the Catholic Church
taught that Mary remained physically a virgin even through the
process of giving birth to Jesus. Mary of Magdala, on the other
hand, arrives on the scene with a fully sexual feminine body.

The Gospel of Philip, one of the Nag Hammadi discoveries, contains an enchanting vignette describing an intimate
relationship between Jesus and the Magdalene: "Jesus loved
her more than most and used to kiss her often."[13] It is hard
not to be bewitched by the tantalizing possibilities that this
conjures up. This passage has been used to suggest that Mary
of Magdala and Jesus were lovers. The textual evidence on the
relationship between Jesus and Mary Magdalene is ambiguous.
It is impossible to prove one way or the other from any known
ancient text that Jesus did or did not have an intimate, even
sexual, relationship with Mary Magdalene — or anyone else.
Some scholars argue that it would have been unorthodox for a
rabbi such as Jesus *not* to have a wife. Others argue that Jesus
was unorthodox in many of his practices and that, because
there is no mention of a wife in the gospel, one did not exist.

When I was teaching theology, students would ask me whether I thought Jesus had ever had sex. Before answering the question, I would always ask them whether or not it would make a difference to their faith if he had, and if so, why? The response, which more often than not was negative, revealed a great deal about the students' ideas about sex and women. For example, they would say that Jesus could never have had sex because it would have demeaned him and sullied the spiritual nature of his mission. Sex would have corrupted Jesus and distracted him from his ministry. Besides, no woman could ever be worthy of being his partner. These were Catholic students who had been raised to believe that priests must be celibate in order to touch the Body of Christ present in the Eucharist. Unlike Protestants, who have married clergy, Catholics believe that a priest must not touch a woman or a man sexually. In other words, they believed that sex and God were inherently incompatible.

There is certainly no historical record to support Dan Brown's contention in *The Da Vinci Code* that the Holy Grail was the Sang Real, or royal bloodline, that originated with a child conceived by Jesus and Mary Magdalene. Nevertheless, popular culture has elevated the fiction to the level of a larger truth: that the Holy Grail is indeed found within a mutuality of love that is both sensual and sacred. *The Da Vinci Code,* with its emphasis on Mary Magdalene's central role in the Christian story, has enjoyed phenomenal success since its publication in 2003. Dan Brown draws on legends of the Grail and the Priory of Sion to weave a story of mystery and intrigue.

Central to the plot is Brown's interpretation of Leonardo da Vinci's *Last Supper*. It is Brown's contention that the figure seated to the right of Jesus in the painting is not the Apostle John but, rather, Mary Magdalene. Clothed in inverse colours — Jesus in a red robe and a blue cloak and the Magdalene in a blue robe and red cloak — they are represented as a pair. In between them is a space, a V-shape that Brown says represents the sacred chalice, the Grail, later revealed to be the female womb. If, as Brown asserts, Mary Magdalene was Jesus' partner, then in Jesus and Mary masculine and feminine are united in a holy union. At the end of the book, the protagonists come to the realization that the Holy Grail is the sacred feminine spirit, suppressed by the Church for almost two thousand years.

Fictional as much of its content may be, *The Da Vinci Code* has created a surge of interest in Mary Magdalene and the earliest era of Christianity. The discovery of suppressed Gnostic texts demonstrates that the exclusion of women from leadership in Christianity represents a departure from its earliest tradition. It was only in the third century that the theological position outlined in the Gnostic texts was rejected, and the Roman church began to emerge as the seat of western orthodoxy. By the fourth century, texts from different authors begin to conflate Mary Magdalene with other women in the gospel. In a sermon he preached in Rome in 593 CE, Pope Gregory the Great associated the figure of Mary Magdalene, apostle to the apostles, with the sinful woman who anointed Jesus with her hair[14] and Mary of Bethany, who anointed

Jesus before his arrest.[15] Mary Magdalene as the repentant whore was to figure prominently in Christian art and imagination until 1969, when the Vatican officially relinquished this interpretation.

So the Roman view of the early church, which favoured the role of Peter and increasingly exalted the position of the Roman pontiffs who were his successors, won out in the struggle for orthodoxy. But now, the rediscovery of the early texts that were ruled out of the canon has brought new life and inspiration to Christianity — inspiration to all who long for an end to the suffocation of the liberating message of Jesus by patriarchal practices in both Catholic and Protestant Christianity. The reinstatement of the sacred feminine as embodied by Mary Magdalene is creating a tantalizing, prophetic image that dances on the margins of the Christian spiritual consciousness. Passionate, creative thinking will lead to a universal spiritual renaissance, inspired by a fresh reading of the scriptures in the light of modern archaeological discoveries, and exposure to other early accounts that were suppressed and then lost for hundreds of years. The early Christian texts uncovered in the twentieth century have captured the collective imagination and could inspire a new era of mutual partnership in the churches and a renewed call for justice for both women and men.

The analysis of the rediscovered texts enables us to draw on traditions from the past to enrich the present. Texts have always been interpreted, but now this interpretation is happening from the margins of religious institutions.

Women have had no power within religious institutions, so they have nothing to lose by opening up and exploring alternative routes to the sacred both inside and outside their respective traditions. That is what is currently occurring in this Magdalene moment. Women are interacting with texts, both old and new, and challenging the dominant interpretations that have prevailed up to the present. Christians are beginning to ponder the enormous significance of what was suppressed by the dominant clerical culture of the past and are becoming receptive to the idea that the spiritual leadership of women alongside men could open up enticing prospects for the future.

New spiritual forces at the margins of the churches are threatening to burst institutional Christianity apart at the seams. The eruption of the feminine at all levels of consciousness is one of these forces. At its core is the Magdalene-inspired movement to examine the role of women in the early church and to draw inspiration from the Gnostic scriptures. Animated by justice from the heart rather than orthodox rules and regulations, this movement will lead to a new partnership of women and men in the church of the future. A Magdalene Christianity would allow what have been peripheral elements — the feminine, the poor, the outcast, the body in all its dimensions (including the erotic), the earth itself — to become central to spiritual consciousness.

The Da Vinci Code has re-ignited debate over the role of women, and the discussion of sexuality in religious practice has intensified. In March 2005, Archbishop Tarcisio Bertone, a former colleague of then Cardinal Josef Ratzinger (the current Pope Benedict XVI) in the Congregation for the Doctrine of the Faith, which monitors theological orthodoxy, advised Catholics not to buy or read *The Da Vinci Code*.[16] This shows just how threatening to the power of the Church is the dispersal of hitherto arcane Gnostic and other gospels to a wider public.

Why is this the case? Because these early Christian writings reveal clearly that the companionship of women was highly valued by Jesus. These texts also show that Mary Magdalene played a key role as the close companion of Jesus and was herself a leader, visionary and healer within the mixed group of men and women who were his closest associates. In his day, Jesus called people who were on the periphery of religious and societal respectability into his inner circle of associates and told them that God regarded them with favour. The Magdalene movement of justice from the heart is one through which God bestows divine grace yet again on the margins of religion and society. In a multiplicity of diverse churches and movements focused on the service of the poor and marginalized, humanity and the earth, there is a rising energy that flows across denominational and religious boundaries. A renewed Magdalene Christianity calls not just for the empowerment of women but also for the embrace of diversity, demanding that we draw strength from vulnerability and non-violence rather than from power and coercion.

Jane Schaberg, Dan Brown and others have claimed that Mary Magdalene was destined to be the true successor to Jesus.

Perhaps that will finally come to pass in our age, two millennia after Jesus walked the earth. It is no coincidence that this is all taking place at this particular time in history. The ever-creative Spirit of God is working to empower men and women inside and outside of religious traditions to wake up and save the planet. The human race is moving into a new awareness of our interconnectedness with the universe. The realization of human kinship with the natural world is growing, and the dangers posed by our depredations of the natural world are gradually being recognized.

The re-emergence of Magdalene Christianity represents a new greening of the original soul of Christianity. The medieval mystic Hildegard of Bingen talks about the "greening" of the soul. According to her, the power within the soul is a life force that transmits the energy of God. Perhaps we can now speak of a greening of the original soul of Christianity as people are inspired by the new possibilities revealed by the rediscovery of texts long buried beneath the earth. At the margins of mainstream churches a fragile but tenacious hope is sprouting. Holding fast to hope does not necessarily mean optimism about the future, because it often requires working within the darkness — the darkness of faith in a future we cannot predict and a God whom we sometimes find it hard to discern. We do not know, except with the power of our intuition and the grace of the Holy Spirit, what shape the future will take. But we do know that we have to burst out of the frozen patterns that are constraining the work of God today.

What are the characteristics of the widening embrace of God, the movement that is stirring up new life on the margins of old traditions? I believe there are four interconnected signs of the Magdalene moment.

First, a revolution in Christian views on women, the erotic and sexual diversity. This begins with the reinstatement of women in leadership, in mutual partnership with men. Imagine if Mary Magdalene, the apostle, had been the driving force behind the early Christian movement. The earliest Christians did indeed place women in roles of leadership. It was later, when the church embraced so much of the ethos of the Roman Empire, that power, status and hierarchies of gender and class became inextricably bound up with its structure.

Conservative Catholic and Protestant fundamentalists are once again trying to put women back into a straitjacket of male supremacy and female subordination, but now they are co-opting feminist language. While they are desperately searching for a return to patriarchal family structure, they are now calling it "complementarity" and presenting it as a pseudo-scientific mandate for the differentiation of male and female roles. But we now know that the construction of gender goes way beyond the biological and, also, that the nature of God is beyond gender. Exciting developments in theology have, moreover, opened new windows onto the feminine in God — and most of this theology is happening beyond the control of the churches. The acceptance of women at all levels of ecclesiastical service is an ongoing development of this new consciousness. When women are recognized not only as fully human but also as able to represent the divine alongside men, then the Holy Spirit will truly have burst the centuries-old bonds of gender.

The embrace of the feminine is connected to the reintegration of the erotic and the sensual into Christian ethics. Christianity has no tradition that sanctifies sexual pleasure. Yet good, mutually pleasurable sex expresses the deepest capacity of the universe for communion and relatedness — God's great gift. Good sex is about justice that is both personal and political — an erotic justice of mutual relationship where good sex releases people's energies for passionate lovemaking and compassionate justice-making.

Good sex is sex that is safe, pleasurable, community-building and conducive to justice.[17] It forges a unity of body and soul that electrifies the soul-force within the body. Good sex results in a "greening" of personal relationships that extends beyond the couple to the earth. Celebrating the power and goodness of desire, taking passionate delight in the body of another and revelling in giving and receiving pleasure can burst us open into a wider existence in which we realize that we were created for communion. Mutual delight is the cradle of intimacy and right relation.

Good lovemaking fuels the passion for equity, and it expresses the yearning for the restoration of oneness within diversity. It subverts the habitually competitive structure of our relationships by reminding us in a very tangible way of our interdependence. A responsible sexual ethic will incorporate erotic power as an essential element of a person's life and ground everything in values of mutual respect and care. A good sexual ethic will raise, not lower, people's expectations.

The Magdalene moment also brings with it the embrace of sexual diversity. Sexual diversity is rooted in the fundamental laws of the universe. Sexual identity is not black and white, but ranges across a spectrum of many shades of feminine and masculine. Gays and lesbians have taken the lead in focusing on sensuality rather than procreation. They have shown the way towards a recognition that diversity, which lies at the heart of the universe, also pertains to sexuality. We also owe a deep gratitude to the courage of gays and lesbians who have spoken out within the churches to fight for justice, especially now, when some right-wing analysts so wrongfully place responsibility for sexual abuse at the door of homosexuals. In order to expand their teachings on sexuality, to centre more on the person rather than on procreation, churches are beginning to listen to the wisdom of the lesbian and gay experience.

The resurrection of the feminine, and the celebration of the erotic and of sexual diversity, are rooted in what some authors now name as the primary sacrament, and what I see as the second major element in this Magdalene moment: the recovery of humanity's connection with creation. The heightened awareness of the earth's interconnected relationships generated by the environmental movement and the new cosmology is the newest and yet most ancient of all revelations of God in our time.

In the words of the scientist and theologian Thomas Berry, at the heart of the earth's configuration lie three fundamental characteristics: interdependence, or communion; diversity, or multiplicity of forms; and subjectivity, or individuality. By communion, Berry means that all the elements of the earth are held together in an interdependent relationship. This relationship does not imply uniformity; quite the opposite. The diversity of life that characterizes creation means that all of earth's elements, down to the smallest atom, are unique, one-of-a-kind. Finally, all of life contains within itself the capacity for self-organization and renewal. As Berry and co-author Brian Swimme write in *The Universe Story*, "Were there no differentiation, the universe would collapse into a homogeneous smudge; were there no subjectivity (autopoesis) the universe would collapse into inert, dead extension; were there no communion, the universe would collapse into isolated singularities of being."[18]

The recovery of the earth, according to Berry, who is also a Catholic priest, is the great work of our age. Berry's books, notably *The Dream of the Earth* and *The Universe Story*, have broken new ground in the relationship of theology to science. Berry and others have recognized that contemporary science has offered religion a new creation story. The fundamental law of the universe is interdependent relationships within a diversity of being. Human sexuality reflects this configuration, which is also exemplified in the Christian Trinitarian understanding of God that places diversity within unity at the very heart of God's being. Creation reflects the image of its creator. As a result of this new partnership between theology and science, a dynamic consciousness of the universe and all that it contains is enriching theology.

The third feature of the Magdalene moment, flowing from the embrace of the earth and the diversity of creation, is a conversion to the simplicity of lifestyle that will lead to a more just social and economic order. The preservation of the delicate ecological balance of the earth demands that people in more affluent countries, most of which have had significant exposure to the Christian tradition, embrace a less materialistic lifestyle. For inspiration, we could look to the women around Jesus, led by Mary Magdalene, who placed their wealth at the service of the common table and thus organized the new economy of the Reign of God preached by Jesus and practised by his community. The apostolic role of the women who relinquished their economic resources was a key component in the early Christian tradition.

Returning to, and broadening, this urgent task of steward-ship of the earth's resources in our time will entail a major shift away from the world of consumerism and a re-emphasis on the common good of humanity, interwoven with that of the earth. International grassroots movements are attempting to curb the drive of global capitalism towards profit at any price, and to provide for a sustainable economic system and a more equable distribution of wealth. Gatherings like the alternative global economic summits held in Porto Alegre, Brazil and Mumbai, India offer signs of hope. Awareness is spreading among consumers in the First World that changes in shopping habits can be instrumental in social change. This has led to boycotts of Nike and other multinational corporations and shows up again in other trends such as the rise in vegetarianism. Young people are leading the way to a simpler lifestyle that will help us to tread more lightly on the earth. My son, a middle-school teacher, became a vegetarian because, he told me, so many of the students in his class were vegetarians that they were putting him to shame.

The final indication of the Magdalene movement and of the revelation of God in our day is the embrace of religious diversity and pluralism. What do the interconnectedness and interdependence of creation point to but a creator God manifest in a rich variety of revelation?

Reciprocity is at the essence of God, according to Christian theology. Reciprocity lies at the foundation of the idea of God as a Trinity of being, a bedrock of Christian belief. Several theologians, among them the late Jacques Dupuis, have produced innovative work on the Trinity and religious pluralism that is opening the door to more interfaith work. Dupuis situates the study of Jesus Christ, or Christology, within Trinitarian theology as a whole, not as a separate component of God: "The Trinitarian model, the universal enlightenment of the Word of God, and the enlivening by his Spirit, make it possible to discover in other saving figures or traditions, truth and grace not brought out with the same vigor and clarity in God's revelation and manifestation in Jesus Christ."[19]

So the revelation of God in Christ is but one aspect of God. God's whole being is greater than the person of Jesus. Thus each religious understanding of God has a unique place in God's plan that is not superseded by the revelation of God within the life and teachings of Jesus. Other religious paths are independent in their own right, with their own God-given goodness and light.

My own doorway into a relationship with God has been opened by Jesus Christ. While my faith in Jesus has faced challenges and undergone transformations over the years, it is still green, still full of sap, still growing. Jesus the Jew dreamt of humanity not divided by tribe, gender, or religion but united in the universal love of God. I believe it is false to his vision to insist, as many Christian churches continue to do, that just because he opened one doorway onto the Trinity, God is bound to receive only those humans who have come through that door. God is always greater than any one religion, or than all religions put together. To teach otherwise is to fall into a form of idolatry.

The dogmatic differences between Catholic and Protestant that caused so much bloodshed at the time of the Reformation now seem far less relevant than the state of the earth and its poorest peoples. We are witnessing the emergence of a post-denominational Christianity in which the praxis of love and life, not the dogmatic difference, is the defining characteristic of the church. A moratorium on missionary activity in all religions is long overdue to diminish the pointless rivalry it engenders. It's time for all the great religions to seek common ground in the search for God. Women are the key to this. Because women have little stake in religious structures, they are freer to move beyond religious institutions in search of new formations.

Christians, in particular, must dismantle the vestiges of empire within the churches and wean them from their secular privileges. Within the Anglican communion, some favour a severing of the Church of England from the monarchy. On the Catholic side, the ability of the Church to witness to the values of Jesus Christ has been compromised by its absorption of the privileges of Roman statehood restored to it by Mussolini's gift of territorial immunity to Vatican City in 1929.

In my wildest moments of hope — call it a pipe dream if you will — I imagine how to remedy this: by moving the Catholic Church out of the Vatican. The United Nations needs a new headquarters off American soil. Vatican City could be given over in trust to the UN, which would then have territorial sovereignty outside the boundaries and governance of the United States. All the treasures of the Vatican Museum could be given to UNICEF to be held in trust for the world's children, to provide money for the work of UNICEF and other UN relief agencies.

The freeing of religions from the trappings of state power is a necessary step along the path to world peace. To live at peace we must face the great challenge of Jesus' teaching: to love the enemy, to welcome the stranger into our space. It is not enough to be against war; we must find ways to include those who have hurt us, personally and politically, within the scope of God's embrace and forgiveness. The embrace of religious pluralism in the interests of peace demands no less. But can historical memories ever be healed?

Viewed against a cosmic backdrop, human history is but a tiny fraction of the magnificent story of the universe that has recently come to light. It was approximately 15 billion years ago that a great explosion of energy sent all the matter that now forms the universe on a fiery journey into the future. But the energy that powered the generation of the elementary particles of matter was also accompanied by the pull toward annihilation. Some elementary particles cohered to form new energy, other clashed, failed to cohere and died. This mysterious process of annihilation and regeneration has continued ever since at every level of life and also in the vicissitudes of human history. "So long as the universe blazes with such energies, this dance in and out of existence continues and would continue for all time ..."[20]

Since the foundation of the universe, the basic forces of positive and negative energy, attraction and repulsion, have been at work. Over the billions of years that creation has evolved, there have been times of great transformation, such as the transition from electrons to the atoms that formed the first galaxies. The stars that once shone so brightly began to slowly collapse in upon themselves and, in their final burst, created the elements out of which the Milky Way was formed. Since then, every development in the chain of evolution has involved a phase shift incorporating annihilation and rebirth.

I believe we are now in the midst of an enormous phase shift in human consciousness that is comparable to the scientific discovery that the earth revolves around the sun.

On the one hand, there is the dying star of patriarchal domination: the belief that the earth and its resources are only transitory and that access to these diminishing resources must be determined by competition rather than cooperation. These beliefs threaten the emerging awareness of the interdependence of humanity and creation. Despite the growing attraction towards a positive planetary consciousness, the negative pull of old hatreds, armed by an untold proliferation of deadly weapons, is edging the planet towards annihilation. Aggressive nationalism and fundamentalist religion are on the rise in many parts of the globe. This is being aided and abetted by the revival of Muslim and Christian ideologies that preach exclusiveness and mutual competition in the name of God. Both of these religions hold to a principle of salvation in a heaven that is by its very nature separated from the created universe.

The reinstatement of the divine feminine calls this belligerent religious antagonism into question. The mutuality of relationship between Jesus the Nazarene and Mary the Magdalene mirrors that fascinating dance between God and Sophia, or Wisdom as portrayed in the biblical Book of Wisdom, where a mysterious co-creative feminine presence appears at the side of God. In this, one of the last texts of the Hebrew Scriptures, we are told that "Wisdom [*sophia* in the Greek] is a reflection of eternal light, a perfect mirror of God's activity and goodness ... more beautiful than the sun and constellations ... living with God, the Lord of all, who loves her ..."[21] This is striking evidence of belief in a feminine aspect of divinity. This late biblical text originated within the community of Greek-speaking Jews resident in Alexandria in the last decades BCE.[22]

Archaeological evidence suggests that long before the Book of Wisdom circulated within the Hellenic world, humans had worshipped divinity under many guises. One of the most ancient was a fertility goddess who was associated with the earth's fruitfulness and with human fertility. With the rise of patriarchy, the divinity of the feminine was suppressed for thousands of years, and women's spiritual status was devalued. We are still living through the end of that period, but I believe that we are on the cusp of a new era in which women and men will be regarded as equal partners, neither one nor the other dominant in the cosmic divine enterprise. The shared creative work of Sophia and Yahweh, the reciprocal energy generated by the Sun and the Moon, the mutual regard of Jesus and Mary Magdalene: thus does God delight in the reciprocal interplay of male and female.

The gathering together of these movements — feminism, sacred sexuality, reverence for creation, and economic and social reform — is part of the Magdalene moment during which new relationships between women and men, humanity and the earth, and God and the universe are being forged. My deepest fear is that we may never fully attain the next phase shift in human consciousness. The ray of hope in all of this is that out of the black hole of despair there could be born, even falteringly, a new constellation whose light will be fuelled by values of justice and cooperation. A change in spiritual values is an intrinsic element of the new constellation, but this is a gamble that is being hazarded against great odds.

I have written this book to add to the sparks of resistance and hope that are fanning out across the globe. In January 2003, Canada and Mexico's refusal to participate in a military invasion of Iraq in the second Gulf War was a defining moment, as both countries took the risk of defying the U.S. government. Local organizations raised awareness, and thousands of people across Canada joined with others in the global community in history's first twenty-four-hour candlelight vigil for peace. This was a Magdalene moment, when those at the margins of power were caught up in a new and powerful solidarity.

In a park in Toronto, just steps from where I had danced with Daniel a few months earlier, I stood on a cold winter's night with about two hundred of my neighbours in a circle warmed by the soft light of hundreds of candles. People spoke spontaneously and passionately about their dream for a better world. Children and dogs played hide-and-seek in and around the unbroken ring of light. A full moon shone above us. At the end, strangers and friends linked arms, reluctant to let go of the intensity of the experience. After I returned home, I thought of the words of the great fourteenth-century Sufi poet Hafiz, a contemporary of Geoffrey Chaucer: "We have not come into this exquisite world / to hold ourselves hostage from love."[23]

Chapter 2

RECLAIMING SEXUALITY

IN THE CELTIC tradition, life is often described as a pilgrimage on the high seas in a small coracle, a light skiff kept afloat by God's love. A heavy cargo of ego and self-righteousness has threatened to sink the little coracle of my life from time to time, but gradually, through patient work, I have been able to lighten the load. My understanding has evolved during periods when I have been stripped of the security of family, status and religion and thrust into new waters, to negotiate ways of navigating in an uncharted ocean. At these moments in my life I have entered into what the Celts call "thin places," where earth and heaven intersect.

At the age of eighteen, I decided to become a nun. In the early 1960s, this was the only way open to Catholic women who wanted to dedicate their lives to God: at that time ordination was not regularly open to women in any Christian church, Catholic or Protestant.

I felt I was entering a different reality — "leaving the world," as it was referred to then. My mother, who was so upset by my decision that she could not bear to be in the house while I was packing, went to Scotland to stay with a friend. A week before my departure, I gathered all my letters and diaries and the mementoes of my childhood and adolescence and burned them in the fireplace. On my last day at home with my family, we ate my favourite dinner of roast chicken, and then I bade them a tearful farewell at London's Victoria Station. I would see them again, but only within the confines of the convent parlour and always in the company of an older nun.

For the first nine months, as one seeking admission to the full program of convent life, I wore the modified habit of a postulant. At the end of this period of scrutiny — which was to determine my suitability to proceed to the next stage of training — I was clothed in a religious habit, entered into the first year of the novitiate and assumed another identity as Sister Mary Jonathan. Towards the end of that year, a fresh group of new postulants crossed the threshold of initiation into convent life. Among them were two women who would also become writers and feminists within different contexts. Teresa Okure was the first African candidate to enter the order: she is now one of the pre-eminent voices of feminist theology in Africa. The other was Karen Armstrong, today one of the world's most celebrated writers on religion. Karen Armstrong, Teresa Okure and I were in the last novitiate cohort to be trained according to the old traditions. All three of us are still engaged in exploring fundamental questions about God, religion, women and the earth.

In the novitiate, each new entrant was assigned a mentor, called a "guardian angel," who would help explain the intricacies of the rules governing convent life. By an extraordinary gift of fate, I was appointed Karen's guardian angel. There must have been a divine irony at work since we both subsequently left the order and became agents for religious change. In her memoir, *The Spiral Staircase*, Karen Armstrong recounts the struggle she faced in adapting to the discipline imposed on us in the novitiate. I remember her fainting spells, which I now realize were attacks of epilepsy. In the book, she describes an incident that involved a spirited exchange between the Mistress of Novices and me. We were discussing the use of guitars to accompany the music of the Mass. An ardent traditionalist, she would not countenance any music other than Gregorian chant or polyphony — both of which I loved. But I also sensed that the Spirit was throwing open the Church's windows to melodies that were more accessible to contemporary youth. I thought we should vary our musical style in order to reach out to them. She disagreed.

A feature of novitiate life was the weekly Chapter of Faults, a dreaded formal convocation where, in the presence of the Mistress of Novices and her deputy, we gathered to confess, on bended knees, any transgressions of the rules committed during the previous week. It was also an opportunity publicly to name faults observed in other novices. At the Chapter of Faults immediately following my challenge to her over the guitars, the Mistress of Novices accused me of arrogance and rewarded my assertiveness with the most severe penance of all: that night at supper, I was to crawl around the refectory on my knees, going under each table to kiss the feet of the nuns seated at supper, about seventy-five in all. Obedience, humility and passivity were the virtues that I was meant to acquire through this penance.

But it had the opposite effect on me. I considered my punishment a sign of honour. It served as a confirmation that I would never allow my spirit to be broken by the more extreme practices of convent life. I knew, then as now, that any attempt to break my spirit by forcing acquiescence imposed by authority rather than the assent of inner conviction ran counter to God's direction of my life. The most rigid aspects of novitiate life were abolished the following year, when I made my vows; we were the last set of nuns ever to be subjected to these severe kinds of punishments. My sojourn at the order's house of studies in London, to which I was then assigned, was an altogether different experience. There I was exposed to the groundbreaking theology of Vatican II. I also began intensive studies in medieval church history at the University of London.

On balance, my years in the convent benefited me greatly. I gained a focus and a pattern of prayer and discipline that have provided a framework within which I can engage the experiences of a life marked by change. My rigorous training in Catholic tradition planted the seeds for my future engagement with theology and feminism. As young nuns, we were encouraged to study theology at the highest levels and taught that women as well as men were expected to carry forward the Church's theological traditions.

Two years into my degree, and seven years after entering the convent, I made the journey back to the world I thought I had renounced forever. I found myself once more in Victoria Station, a small suitcase in hand, clad again in "worldly" clothes. I then embarked on the short but momentous train ride back to my childhood home.

My decision to leave was motivated by the desire to marry a young Jesuit, the first great love of my life, whom I had met at university when we were both studying medieval history. Roger and I attended the same seminars and critiqued each other's essays. He taught me to play chess in the rose garden of London University's Bedford College. It was not long before other moves were initiated by our awakening sexual desire. We eventually decided to marry.

I spent a year in agonizing deliberation before reaching that final decision. How could I, called by God to be the Bride of Christ, now renounce my heavenly bridegroom for an earthbound one? Nuns were the chosen brides of Christ and our virginity was offered in self-surrender to this divine bridegroom. Before I left the cloister, I went on an eight-day silent retreat. I stood in front of a life-size crucifix in the convent garden and prayed for direction. None came.

Much later I realized that my decision to leave the convent marked an important step into adult faith — a faith found not in certainty and light, but in ambivalence and darkness.

Trust in God depends on living through times when the view ahead is murky, the path is new and all the usual signposts that mark the way have been torn down. At such times we perceive that God erupts through the unexpected cracks in our shattered self-reliance, like the molten core of fire at the centre of the planet.

It took me some time to set aside the idea that God had loved me more when I was celibate. The Catholic Church teaches that the less sexual you are, the closer you are to God. Sexless and therefore pure angels surround the thrones of Jesus and Mary. The perpetual virginity of Mary the Madonna is still held up for veneration. Even sex within marriage was, until very recently, considered holier if it was directed towards procreation rather than pleasure.

Since sexual attraction had factored in my decision to leave the convent, my superiors within the order showed their disapproval by concealing my plans from the other nuns. My trunk was kept in the basement of the convent, and I was forced to creep up and down the back stairs in the middle of the night to pack my meagre belongings. In the early hours of a bright summer morning, I closed the front door in total silence, forbidden to say goodbye to any of my friends. Only Dorothy, a senior nun and university professor who had befriended me, accompanied me first to Mass in Westminster Cathedral and then to Victoria Station. I left with her the half-dozen letters I had written to my close friends who remained behind. All but two of them also eventually left the order.

My mother was overjoyed and welcomed me with open arms when I arrived back home. When Roger and I married two years later, I thought I was ready for my new life. I looked forward to starting my first teaching job, to having children, and to settling down into a predictable pattern of marriage and family life as I had experienced it within my own family. Little did I know that the small coracle of my life was about to weigh anchor and set out on another unpredictable voyage, this time with no map or stars to navigate by.

Roger and I had left religious life at a crucial point in the history of the Catholic Church, which also coincided with a period of profound social change. The 1960s marked the end of the Church Triumphant, the outlook that ruled Catholicism when we had joined the priesthood and convent respectively. From the late 1960s into the 1970s the Church was trying to find common ground with the modern world on its own terms. Pope John XXIII opened the door for Catholics to receive wisdom from secular experience, and an unprecedented exchange between the world and the Church began. Vatican II allowed people to stop for a moment and imagine a different kind of Church, one that broke down the walls of the fortress against the outside world erected over the course of previous centuries. Through the gaps in the walls of the fortress would emerge a humbler, pilgrim Church that would journey in solidarity with the rest of humankind, especially the poorest. The Church seemed poised on the threshold of a major re-evaluation of its previously held prejudices against other Christians and other religions.

And, not least, its teachings on the nature and role of women came under scrutiny.

During my seven years in the convent, marriage and women's roles in the world had entered a period of extreme flux. As a young wife with a career I was woefully unprepared to step into the minefield of emerging feminist awareness. Women and men of my generation were experiencing break-neck change, and I was about to become painfully aware of this. Marriage and family in the 1970s were not what they had been when I was growing up, or even what they had been for my older sisters.

As university students who were both in religious life, Roger and I had begun our relationship as equals. We had shared the same tutorials, and our intellectual and spiritual lives had overlapped within a common ground of mutual respect. Yet our marriage plunged us into traditional gender roles. I became a wife, he a husband. Neither of our families provided models for a two-career marriage with equal distri-bution of responsibilities. Instead of equally matching us on the chessboard, the strategy of this new game of equal marriage would mean making new moves out of centuries of tradition in which women had been checkmated at every turn. I had started to work full-time, but when babies came along, I was also expected to shoulder the additional care for the house and the children.

Many women and men of my generation share this experi-ence. Though we were among the earliest to benefit from the widespread distribution of the pill, so that we didn't have children immediately after marriage and had some choice and control over the spacing of our families, daycare was still frowned on. When children were born there was a whole new raft of responsibilities to cover. Two-career families were a new phenomenon. Individual men were not the problem; it was the unexamined sexism that had hitherto conditioned the culture. But when traditional gender roles were at stake within a relationship, it was hard to separate the personal from the systemic. In a two-career family, who would prepare the supper, bathe and put the children to bed, and clean the house? Even with the best of intentions, we wrestled with these concrete issues almost every day.

When we moved to Toronto in the late 1970s, I went back to school to take a master's course in theology and education. As I delved further into liberation theology and feminist theory, I began to understand how a confluence of culturally and religiously conditioned gender roles had affected my own life. I realized to what extent religion had reinforced and perpetuated the dominance of men in all spheres of life. Despite Vatican II, the Catholic Church was still promoting gender stereotypes of male and female roles within marriage: men should go out to work, and women should stay home to care for the family. When I began to teach at the Faculty of Education at York University in the 1980s, I discovered that many of my adult students were going through a similar reappraisal of their relationships and roles.

Then the scandals of sexual abuse of children by Catholic priests hit the North American press. I have described the impact of this in my previous books. Over twenty-five years have passed since the first media exposure of widespread child abuse in the Catholic Church. Since that time, in Boston and elsewhere in the United States, and in parishes and seminaries throughout the Catholic world, the grisly details of organized rings of pedophiles and purveyors of child pornography have continued to come to light. The abuse of children was one great sin that Jesus judged with unmitigated severity: "Anyone who abuses one of these little ones who believe in me, it were better for him that a millstone be hanged around his neck and that he were drowned in the depths of the sea."[1] The apathy of so many Catholics in the face of this scandal, and their willingness passively to continue going to church on Sunday without demanding reforms in the system that protected and even indulged the perpetrators of these terrible crimes, were simply incomprehensible to me. And I was not alone.

For a few years, lay Catholics in Canada rallied in support of the victims and called for reform of the church. By a combination of circumstances, I along with many others called for changes in the structures of the Church that would lead to more transparency and accountability. But the impact of my public role of critic of the Church proved to be the straw that broke the camel's back in my marriage. Like my decision to leave the convent, the separation was a wrenching decision made within another dark night of the soul. I was wracked with apprehension about the possible effects on our two teenaged sons.

I had lost a marriage, and I was losing a church. How could I continue to sing the song of the Lord in an institution where the crimes committed against children cried out to heaven for vengeance? How could I offer my gift at the altar when the Eucharist in the Catholic Church was celebrated in a context of such profound injustice, against both women and children? Awakened to a new and painful awareness of the sexism and denial rife within the structures of the Church, I entered a period of exile. I was sustained during this time by women's house churches, as well as small groups where others who had also entered into the wilderness gathered to break the bread of life.

I now realize that this period of flight from the institutional Church drew me closer to the great work that God is doing in our time. I had been pushed to the very edge of Catholicism, but in what at first appeared to be a spiritual desert, I was sustained by the company of other Christians living in communities of recovery on the margins of Christianity.

The account in the Book of Exodus of the flight of the Israelites from slavery in Egypt and their forty-year sojourn in the desert is one of the foundational archetypes of personal and communal religious identity. Once they had passed through the Red Sea and entered the Sinai desert, the Israelites had no food other than the manna that rained down from the sky each morning, "thin and flaky and delicate as frost."[2] The story has much to teach us about the sustainability of creation and economic systems, themes that I will explore in later chapters. But while I was psychologically and spiritually in recovery from religious absolutism, I was often sustained by delicate reminders from God that I was on the right path.

The breakdown of what I had thought would be a life-long marriage also found me facing dilemmas about gender identity. Not only had I failed as a nun, but while I was married I had often sensed that I did not fit into the ideal of traditional femininity. Now I felt that I had failed as a wife and as a mother too. I was not just a nun who had left the convent. Now that I had broken a second set of vows, I didn't fit within any of the approved religious categories. And yet I had wanted nothing more than to be a good wife and mother, have a satisfying career as a teacher and remain involved with the Church.

In the wake of my divorce, the insights of feminist theology and my deepening relationship with God through contemplative prayer had opened the eyes of my soul to a depth of being at my core that was dynamic and energizing. I gained a new understanding of the connection between women's strength and women's sensuality. At the same time that I became more committed to the struggle for women's equality, I embarked on a short-lived relationship with a man. For someone who had been a virgin before marriage and had never been unfaithful in the course of nineteen years of married life, this was truly an audacious move. This short but sweet relationship was deeply healing. Though transient, it restored my confidence in myself as a sexual being. When I sat down to pray, I would laugh at the incongruity of what was going on.

But through the warmth of these sexual experiences, I came to feel the care and affection of God cradling me with loving arms during an extremely difficult time in my life.

What I had stumbled upon was good sex outside a religiously sanctioned relationship. Scratch the surface and most adults will admit to similar experiences. Generations of Catholics have been made frigid by the fear of sex. But contact with the divine source of eros in a context of mutual love and respect releases what is best in the human heart; it does not constrain it. To rise from a loving embrace to face another day intensifies the drive to go forth and renew the earth, comfort its peoples and purify its waters. It is an incentive to reach out and allow others to participate in the healing that loving and intimate touch bestow. In this world of so much sorrow, to reach heaven for a few moments in the arms of a beloved partner is indeed a source of profound joy. Psalm 84 expresses it so beautifully: "My heart and my flesh sing for joy ... as we go through the bitter valley we make it a fountain of springs."

Sexual intimacy is a sign that God still cherishes us during times of vulnerability and uncertainty. Sex can assuage a whole gamut of human needs. Making love can lead to reconciliation for a couple, in situations where further words would serve only to wound. At other times, the intensity of sex can convey sparks of the originating burst of energy that gave birth to the universe. It can lead us to the heart of God, who is the creative male and female energy at the core of each of us. But because sex is so powerful, it can be the source of terrible suffering and pain as well as joy. The appalling suffering inflicted on women and children in the pursuit of self-centred sexual gratification, and the sexual exploitation and trafficking of poor women and children, have increased exponentially with globalization and internet communication. The commercialization of sex has led to situations where sexual permissiveness has caused untold grief.

The Church's obsession with controlling sex has resulted both in unhealthy fear and in fascination. Centuries of religious censure — fuelled by the fear of female sexual pleasure and orgasm — have haunted the Christian religious imagination. Ever since the author of the First Letter to Timothy asserted that childbearing redeemed the sinful nature of women,[3] female sexual desire disengaged from procreation has been suspect. It is hard to break through centuries of patriarchy to articulate a spirituality of mutually pleasurable, healthy sex, just as it is risky to proclaim that message in a secular context where it may be misunderstood as an invitation to unfettered promiscuity. The recognition of sex as an essential, natural part of who we are, and therefore a gift from God, has not been a feature of the Christian tradition, present though it is in the Hebrew Scriptures. The rare and overtly sexual imagery in the Song of Songs, for example, has been spiritualized into representing the mystical love between God and the soul.

The ideals of good sex cannot be effectively inculcated by celibates, especially those who have been forced into celibacy as a condition of ordination to the Catholic priesthood. If one of your main struggles in life is how to control your sexuality, then this will invariably colour your understanding of sex. Your main focus — unsurprisingly — is how to avoid sex altogether, or if you are involved in an illicit sexual liaison, how to extricate yourself from it. This is hardly the best physical, mental or spiritual environment from which to transmit a healthy attitude towards sex. A true theology of sex would stress that spiritual integrity and maturity are achieved through sex rather than in spite of it. Good sex is a partnership that involves giving as well as receiving; it overflows into the rest of life, into a feeling that the world would be a better place if we took more care of one another on a greater scale.

Many mystics use sexual imagery to describe their experience of prayer. Physical sex can be a gateway into the depths of the soul, into transformative prayer. Meditation after sex can transmit the afterglow of orgasm to the fire of contemplation. Far from presenting a barrier to union with God, good sex fosters openness to the Spirit. It breaks down the barriers between the divine and the human by opening up the vulnerable area, deep within our being, to trust.

I have come to appreciate that gays and lesbians manifest in a unique way the creative energy of God. They represent God's supreme freedom to draw outside the lines of what religion has insisted are mutually exclusive boundaries of male and female. For Christians, a deeper perception of the mystery of the Trinitarian God can lead to an appreciation of sexual diversity. The mystery of the diversity of existence within the triune divine nature is the foundation of our belief. God at once embraces every possibility of being but cannot be reduced to any particular prototype, whether this be male or female, gay or straight. The elusive diversity of one God in three persons cannot be neatly categorized by any human standard of measurement. Likewise humans, made in the image of God, do not fit into clearly demarcated categories. This is a real gift for all who have the eyes to see it.

Mystics, such as the fourteenth-century English recluse Julian of Norwich, relate insights from their deep contemplation that challenge a comfortable, everyday understanding of God. How else can Julian describe Jesus as our mother as well as our brother — something that we can understand but can't explain? "And although our earthly mother may suffer her child to perish, our heavenly Mother Jesus may never suffer us who are his children to perish, for he is almighty, all wisdom and all love, and so is none but he, blessed may be he …"[4] Julian's *Revelations* speak of the kindness of a Mother and Father God who, in a wonderfully womanly way, knits us into one pattern with the Trinity. "The high might of the Trinity is our Father," she writes, "and the deep Wisdom of the Trinity is our Mother, and the great love of the Trinity is our Lord: and in our human creation we have all these three properties of the Trinity."[5]

The idea of God as a Trinity of being represents a primordial breaking of all barriers. A triune God can never be separated from a multiplicity of divine identities, each individually complete yet each inextricably linked to the other. Jesus' release of the Holy Spirit at Pentecost deepens the human understanding of God as it evolves across the centuries of prayer and experience. The Holy Spirit continually opens our minds to new understanding. The Trinity is not a closed dogma, but one that is always revealing new insights.

To cross gender barriers is to rediscover the diversity that is within the nature of God. Jesus himself has been called a "theological transvestite." I came across this phrase recently in *The Resurrection of Mary Magdalene,* where Schaberg quotes a Jewish feminist writer, Susannah Heschel.[6] Heschel uses the symbol of transvestitism to argue that Jesus destabilizes all human boundaries, particularly those that exist between Judaism and Christianity.[7] Encountering a transvestite causes a suspension of disbelief and challenges conventional gender definitions.

I remember my first close encounter with transvestites. It was at a nightclub in Toronto, and I was with a young gay friend. I had a wonderful time — dancing to my heart's content and enjoying the freedom of not being the focus of any man's desire. At one point I went to the women's washroom and was suddenly faced with a group of transvestite dancers applying their makeup. Once I got over the initial shock, I found myself captivated by their beauty and grace — a beauty that defied categorization. It was a startling and powerful experience that challenged me to question my own assumptions about gender.

In his life, Jesus transgressed many boundaries, religious and otherwise. The very fact that God stepped into human history crosses the threshold of our human understanding of the divine. Jesus' incarnation — God becoming human —

is itself an act of transvestitism: flesh for Jesus was like a new garment that both reveals and conceals God's nature. He remained a Jew to the end and yet he is acknowledged as the founder of Christianity. As soon as we try to define him we cease to do justice to the mystery of his multi-faceted presence with us, both then and now. Hence his poignant remark in the Gospel of Luke about the fickleness of human favour. People criticize him because he eats and drinks freely, but they rejected John the Baptist because he fasted too strictly. Jesus feels like a wedding singer who plays the flute in the marketplace; not many people recognize the music, let alone dance to it.[8]

The image of Jesus has been overlaid for so long with the garments of celibacy and masculinity that we have lost sight of the remarkable balance of male and female qualities he displayed. He upheld compassion and abhorred violence. He cared for and nurtured children. He engaged a Samaritan woman in a theological discussion. He enjoyed the company of prostitutes and sinners, and not just for the purposes of preaching to them. He fed people, washed their feet, and wept openly. In the end, he was put to death by the Pharisees, the Religious Right of the day, in alliance with the Roman imperial military. His life suggests manifold ways of living outside the boundaries of gender stereotypes.

Jesus was physical with people beyond the norms of his culture, which frowned upon physical contact with the sick for fear of religious contamination. He was acutely aware of the slightest touch, even to the hem of his garment.

He scandalized apostles and Pharisees alike by allowing a woman to dry his feet with her hair.

Jesus often acted in ways that were inconsistent with what people expected God to do. He didn't punish sin; he forgave it. He didn't observe the rules of religious purification concerning eating, but sat down with the ritually unclean. He brought the unwashed multitude into the inner courts of the temple. Jesus changed our understanding of what is pleasing to God: not the harsh ritual of animal sacrifices, but the purity of an open and compassionate heart. By comforting the afflicted, he also afflicted the comfortable.

If there is one boundary to be drawn by the followers of Jesus, it is a boundary of love against hate. In the pursuit of love, Jesus dances around and across the borders of every fence that humans have tried to erect in his name. He continues to play the flute in the marketplace, but unfortunately many still do not join the dance. The mainstream churches have been notoriously flat-footed in taking up Jesus' invitation to step into the unknown. Some churches have even become agents in mobilizing collective bigotry in order to shut the dance down altogether.

If we truly believe that through baptism, as Paul tells us in his Letter to the Galatians, we have all "put on Christ and we are no longer male nor female, rich nor poor, slave nor free but one humanity in Christ," then all boundaries of gender, class, religion and sexual orientation are blown away in the mighty wind of the divine Spirit.[9] To follow this teaching, we must open our lives to embrace those who differ from us.

I have learned much about sex and identity from gay and lesbian friends. And though shunned by so many churches, gays and lesbians are often among the most devout believers.

This Magdalene moment calls for the courage to live *now* in a new world in which male and female — and every variation thereof — are reconstituted and celebrated. The longing deep in the human heart for intimate union and mutually significant relationships mirrors the pattern imprinted on every particle of the cosmos for mutuality within diversity. This longing has been perverted over the centuries by both religious sanctions against sex for pleasure and the pornographic use of sex for power. One has produced a crippling sense of guilt, the other an excess of promiscuous narcissism.

We live in an interdependent universe. Sex is one of the profoundest expressions of the self-giving, self-transcending love that is a fundamental characteristic of creation. One dimension of the task of our age is to link eros and earth: teaching our children that mutual respect for a partner and a deeply satisfying bodily union must overflow into care for the body of the earth and all its creatures. This is an ennobling vision for sexual healing and health.

The creation of a family, whether biological, adopted or extended, is an expression of hope for the future of the planet. A new appreciation of the role of women, gays and lesbians is one of the most precious signs of the Magdalene moment in Christianity. If we are to follow the example of Jesus, Christianity should know no boundaries. The admission of Gentiles to baptism, recounted in the fifteenth chapter of the

Book of Acts, set the paradigm for an inclusive and evolving church. At crucial moments in the history of Christianity, boundaries have been courageously transgressed. There is usually a fight — factions develop, and some people threaten to leave.

In our own times, the ordination of women has caused rifts and factions within the Catholic Church. I remember the first time I saw a woman at the altar in an Anglican Church in full vestments. It startled me, and then took my breath away by its beauty. This battle over the full equality of women, already won in the majority of Protestant churches, remains volatile in Catholicism primarily because of the linked issue of celibacy. Ever since Pope Gregory VII introduced the policy of celibacy in the eleventh century, women have not been included in Catholic priests' households other than as cooks or cleaners.

In the beginning it was not so. Women and men, married and single, worked and travelled side by side to preach, heal and found small Christian communities. Mary Magdalene, as we have seen, played a crucial role in this development. But over the course of time, the Virgin Mary came to supersede the Magdalene as the pre-eminent role model for Christian women. For centuries, the Virgin Mary, Mother of God, and Mary Magdalene have been used to perpetuate stereotypes about the place of women in Christian societies around the world. Deconstructing these stereotypes is crucial to understanding and re-evaluating both the role of women in religious leadership and the attitudes within Christianity towards sex.

The image of the Virgin Mother that the male Church gradually superimposed on Mary floated down through the centuries on a cloud of surreal femininity and suppressed sexuality. The Virgin Mary became the celibate ideal of perfect womanhood. She was meek and obedient. And she was sexless. The maternal but asexual figure of the Madonna has provided a safe repository for the projection of repressed desire onto a woman who came to symbolize the eternal feminine. This miraculous woman, who had a baby while retaining her virginity, is safely beyond the reach of lust.

Catholic women's sexuality has for centuries been regulated by this ideal of the asexual mother. The stereotype of the Virgin Mary meek and mild has done untold damage to women by creating an ideal they can never attain. Women who do not fit this image of Mary — the perfect virgin who is also a fruitful mother — have been held responsible for creating sexual temptation and thus bringing about the fall of men from grace.

A woman whom the feminist theologian Marcella Althaus-Reid describes as "going to bed with God while avoiding full sex" has been held up as the role model for women.[10] Women have been inhibited from inaugurating serious theological reflection about their bodies and their sexuality because the feminine role model is a woman whose only bodily function is to give birth. Traditional Marian teaching has disembodied theology by negating sexuality. Sexuality is celebrated only when it is directed towards procreation. Mary's womb and sometimes her breasts are objects of Catholic devotion, which remains silent on other parts of her body.

According to Elisabeth Schüssler Fiorenza, another contemporary feminist theologian, the cult of the Virgin Mary in Catholic theology has devalued the lives of real women in three ways. "First, by emphasizing virginity to the detriment of sexuality; second, by unilaterally associating the ideal of 'true womanhood' with motherhood; and thirdly, by religiously valorizing obedience, humility, passivity and submission as the cardinal virtues of women."[11] In the same paragraph, Schüssler Fiorenza quotes American writer Mary Gordon, who relates that, "in my day Mary was a stick to beat smart girls with. Her example was held up constantly: an example of silence, of subordination, of the pleasure of taking the back seat."

In an effort to suppress the fundamental role played by women in early Christianity, the patriarchal church for centuries set up the Virgin Mary and Mary Magdalene in opposition as two extremes of female identity: virgin mother or repentant whore. Catholic women who now seek equal access to all the sacraments of the Catholic Church, including ordination, have been barred by the Vatican on the grounds that being a priest would be false to their Marian and maternal nature. The level of motherhood to which the church exalts them does not, however, permit them to attain the governance of "Mother Church."

The lack of a Christian theology that fosters a positive sexual role model for women has reinforced cultural patterns for men and women. Young men whom I taught in a Catholic high school told me that they fully expected to get their first sexual experiences by sleeping around with girls they defined as sluts. But when it came to marriage, their brides had to be virgins. Many cultures attach an economic value to virgins as "unspoiled" property to be transferred from one family to another in the marriage contract. I encountered many male Catholic teens who admitted to engaging in premarital sex themselves yet objected vociferously to their sisters' doing likewise.

Following the efforts of more than a generation of women working in theological studies, the lives of the two Marys are now enjoying a renaissance of interpretation, which has the potential to empower women, promote them to positions of leadership in the churches and free all Christians from the bonds of sexual repression and guilt. This is difficult and controversial work because theological analysis by and about women has been preceded by centuries of institutional and patriarchal interpretation of the texts and stories.

It is now widely accepted that both Marys were founders of Christianity and sisters in the work of the Spirit. Now that women are pursuing theological studies, their explorations of the role of women in the gospels have opened up vital new insights into how the later curtailment of the role of women within Christianity has distorted the practice of Jesus. Women, hitherto mere consumers of male theology, are now becoming producers, active in the transformation of teachings that have hitherto devalued and limited their role. In the course of teaching I frequently came across Catholic girls who are reshaping the tradition in ways more attuned to their contemporary experience of women's empowerment.

Some years ago I took a leave of absence to run a high-school retreat program at Sanctuary, an inner-city Christian outreach centre in Toronto. The program aimed to bring the Christian faith to life for students by sending them out onto the streets of the city with their minds and hearts open to the characters and situations that appear in the parables of Jesus. When they first arrived, they were divided into small groups, with each group assigned a passage from the gospels to read and take with them.

Accompanied by an adult guide, the groups would then set off for a destination where they would meet and interact with marginalized people. The locations they visited included a drop-in for the homeless or the mentally challenged, a shelter for abused women, a centre for the relief of people with AIDS, and a hostel for refugees. In the afternoon, the students would discuss and pray about their experiences and then present skits to the rest of the group.

Among the places they visited was Sojourn House, a shelter and immigration centre for refugees. The reading assigned to this particular location was taken from the Gospel of Matthew: "After the wise men had left, an angel of the Lord appeared to Joseph in a dream and said, 'Herod will be looking for the child in order to kill him. So get up, take the child and his mother, and escape into Egypt, and stay there until I tell you to return.' So Joseph got up right away, took the child and his mother and left in the middle of the night for Egypt where they stayed until Herod died."[12]

At Sojourn House, the students heard first-hand accounts of the civil wars, ethnic conflicts and religious persecutions that had caused people to flee, many in the middle of the night with just the clothes on their backs, to seek safety in Canada. One day, the students who had visited Sojourn House presented a dramatic interpretation of the Holy Family's flight into Egypt, based on the treatment some refugee claimants had received at the Canadian or U.S. border. Mary and Joseph, refugee claimants arriving with their baby at the Egyptian border, were confronted by Egyptian immigration officers.

The student who took the role of Mary was a vibrant, self-confident girl. She sported a nose ring and a crown of pink spiky hair. She opened the skit, the infant Jesus in her arms, arriving with Joseph at the Egyptian border to claim refugee status. The students playing the immigration officers framed their questions to show the contemporary prejudices often displayed towards refugees and immigrants. "Why should our taxes be used to support your kid? Aren't you just here to take advantage of Egypt's welfare system and free health care? How many so-called relatives of yours are you going to bring here after you?" At a couple of points, Mary pounded the table with her fist and shouted at the border guards. She, her child and her man, Joseph, she insisted, were fleeing death squads and desperately needed shelter. If they were turned back, they faced certain execution. In no uncertain terms, she outlined why they deserved asylum.

In the discussion afterward, some of the group commented that this portrayal of Mary was much more aggressive than the Virgin's traditional image. The student who had played Mary stood up, legs slightly apart and fists clenched. "This Mary," she declared, "has brass knuckles!" As liberation theologians have pointed out, this portrayal is actually closer to the real Mary of the gospels than the more recent model of subservient womanhood. At the time of the flight into Egypt, Mary was not yet twenty. She lived in occupied territory in Palestine, whose king was an ally of the Roman colonizers, and she was forced to flee to save her life and that of her infant son. No wonder she needed metaphorical brass knuckles.

Mary's longest recorded statement, the Magnificat, placed on her lips by Luke the evangelist, is one of the most powerful and assertive statements in the Bible. God, proclaims Mary, will cast down the mighty ones from their thrones, scatter the proud in their conceits, and send the rich away empty-handed.

Mary with Brass Knuckles! I longed for an artist to appear, a modern Leonardo or Raphael, someone who could paint her. This Mary of the Magnificat, defender of the children of the poor, also brought to mind the image of the goddess Minerva at the pool in Bath, where nursing mothers had left offerings in the shape of breastplates, symbolizing her protective care of them and their children.

The Magnificat uttered by Mary with Brass Knuckles is a leap of faith, calling on a God who sees life from the vantage of the poor. In Jesus' teaching also, God demonstrated that access to the sacred does not run through the traditional patriarchal family. God's favour rests not with the high priest Zachariah but with the women in his family who, at least on the surface, have placed themselves outside patriarchal religious rules and control. In the opening chapter of Luke's gospel, the pregnant Mary journeys alone to visit her cousin Elizabeth, who is also pregnant. Mary has no male protector or guardian and Elizabeth's husband, the high priest Zachariah, has been struck dumb for doubting the message that he and his wife would become parents in their old age. At the very outset of the Christian story, it is women who assume responsibility for the work of God. Women, likewise, feature prominently at the end, within the drama of the crucifixion and Christ's resurrection. It is only now that their unique contributions have been freed from negative sexual stereotypes to frame the gospel story within a feminine symmetry.

The uniqueness of Mary Magdalene consists in the integration of the sexual, the sacred and spiritual leadership. For too long, Mary Magdalene's role has been distorted by sexual stereotyping. Feminist scholars have been responsible for her reinstatement as an apostolic leader but have resisted attempts to forge an erotic link between the Magdalene and Jesus. Their caution is well founded. To give prominence to Mary Magdalene primarily as the wife or partner of Jesus would merely be to replace her negative sexual stereotype with a positive one. The Gospel of Mary, while delineating the close relationship between Mary Magdalene and Jesus, also clearly argues that leadership should be based on spiritual maturity, regardless of gender.

Resexualizing Mary Magdalene is certainly a pitfall to be avoided if this detracts from her capacity to stand alone in her own right. But neither should we go to the other extreme and allow the struggle for women's spiritual equality to preclude the erotic. Much of the remedy for this confusion lies in acknowledging the possibility of a sexually active Jesus. This would augment our appreciation of his humanity and help to release the body and all its beauty from the ambivalence in which it has languished within Christian teaching. Sex has for too long been viewed as inimical to spiritual progress. By honouring the flesh as sacred we affirm the sacredness of creation. A new soul-force of energy is generated within the body, and heaven is reconnected with earth.

The Earth
Lifts its glass to the sun
And light — light
Is poured.

A bird
Comes and sits on a crystal rim
And from my forest cave I
Hear singing,

So I run to the edge of existence
And join my soul in love.

I lift my heart to God
And grace is poured.

An emerald bird rises from inside me
And now sits
Upon the Beloved's
Glass.

I have left that dark cave forever.
My body is blended with His.

I lay my wing
As a bridge to you

So that you can join us
Singing.

— FROM HAFIZ, "A CRYSTAL RIM" [13]

Chapter 3

THE FIRE AT THE HEART
OF CREATION

WHEN I WAS a young nun, I came across the writings of Pierre Teilhard de Chardin during a retreat. As I read *Hymn of the Universe* in the deep silence of those eight days set aside for contemplation, a resonance with his work filled my whole body with song. Energy coursed through my veins, and a tingle moved up my spine: a sensate response of the body in harmony with the spirit. Teilhard frequently experienced this wild and uncontrollable joy of the spirit-body connection when he celebrated the Eucharist: "May this communion of bread with the Christ clothed in the powers which dilate the world free me from my timidities and heedlessness! ... The one who is filled with an impassioned love of Jesus hidden in the forces which bring increase to the earth is the one that the earth will lift up like a mother in the immensity of her arms, and will enable him to contemplate the face of God."[1]

The body of Christ is offered as sustenance for the world, and is one with the earth.[2] The human spirit is strengthened by the power that flows out of the mothering embrace of the earth. The passion and energy to do good work in the world come from a combination of spirituality with sensuality. Prayer permeated with sensuality at the same time demands a fierce asceticism that cordons off the heart in order to focus attention completely on the divine presence within and without. This is a paradox that is only grasped in the doing of it. My Catholic upbringing, with worship embedded within a setting of flowers, incense, soaring architecture and music, drew me to God through sensual threads. When I later discovered the unique and deep intimacy of a sexual relationship, it became another celebration of divine goodness coursing through the body, from the deepest feelings of the heart to the tiny erections of hairs on the arms. All is electrified with a divine chorus that shouts "yes" in a great amen of transcendent power.

I first encountered Teilhard's writings in the 1960s, before an awareness of either the environmental crisis or the implications of quantum physics had become part of the public domain. A Jesuit priest, paleontologist, mystic and philosopher who lived from 1881 to 1955, Teilhard was one of the first creative thinkers to articulate the connection between theology and the new cosmology. But his ideas, like Galileo's, threatened the status quo. He was forbidden by the Catholic Church to teach or publish his ideas. His work drew the ire of the Church because it challenged the dualistic distinction between the material and spiritual world that had been incorporated into

Catholic theology from Greek philosophy. Teilhard's conception of the universe was dynamic, not static. He perceived
that the universe is not an empty space between heaven
and earth, but is alive and active. At the heart of the material
universe lies a "planetary thinking network," an interlinked
system of consciousness of which humanity is the self-aware
component.[3]

His convictions about human evolution led him to revisit
the traditional notion of original sin. He realized that human
sinfulness could not have been the result of a single act by the
first human couple because, according to evolutionary theory,
such a couple could not have existed. Rather, to Teilhard, the
sinful traits of humans stem from the fact that we exist in an
ever-changing, dynamic and unfinished cosmos, where we
have the capacity to inflict grievous harm. He believed that
humanity and the universe were in process, moving from chaos
and evil to order and perfection. The fusion of theological and
scientific insight in Teilhard's thought brought a new level of
depth to his prayer and his celebration of the sacraments. The
vitality of the inorganic and organic material world, alive with
the creative energy of God in evolution, released his theology
from the rigid division between earth — the transitory and
sin-laden material universe —and the spiritual, perfect and
otherworldly heavenly space where God dwells. For Teilhard
the material world, already alive with God's energy within
all its life forms, has been further penetrated by the added
divine power of Christ's resurrected Eucharist. So the whole
earth becomes the body of Christ, both suffering and joyful,

which humans have been called to reverence and celebrate. "By virtue of the Word's immersion in the world's womb the great waters of the kingdom of matter have, without even a ripple, been imbued with life."[4]

In his exhilarating "Mass on the World," written in 1923, Teilhard celebrates the fire of Christ's love and presence, which penetrates every fibre of being in the universe, yet without consuming it. "All things individually and collectively are penetrated and flooded by the Fire; from the tiniest atom to the mightiest sweep of the most universal laws of being ... the cosmos has burst spontaneously into flame."[5] For Teilhard, God is the divine milieu in which the universe emerges. Every place in the universe is part of God's living body. God is not identified with the universe, but the universe is rather a sacrament and revelation of God.

"A breeze passes in the night. When did it spring up? Whence does it come? Whither is it going? No one knows. No one can compel the Spirit, the gaze of the light of God, to descend upon him. On some given day, someone suddenly becomes conscious of being alive to a particular perception of the divine spread everywhere about. Question him. When did this state begin? He cannot tell. All that he knows is that a new spirit has entered into his life."[6]

One of the most urgent tasks of our present moment in history is to uncover the sacredness of creation, the holiness in the world, in water, sun and forest, and in our own bodies, and accord all of this with due honour as a living manifestation of God's presence. Late arrivals on earth, we humans have evolved over eons, from the ancient amphibians that first crawled onto the land to the dominant species that we have become. But we have cut ourselves off from our origins and forgotten that our roots lie deep within the earth and that through creation we are linked to God.

In the first chapter of the Book of Genesis, creation stirs with life as the Spirit of God hovers over the waters. The Hebrew word for God used in this passage is *ruach*, which means wind or breath. The gender of the noun *ruach* is feminine as well as masculine. This breath of the Spirit is the "wild air, world-mothering air, nestling me everywhere" of Gerard Manley Hopkins ("The Blessed Virgin Compared to the Air We Breathe"). This mothering God broods over the nascent creation, pondering perhaps the beauty that she will bring forth. She is that "Holy Ghost," to continue with Hopkins' poetic insight again, who "over the bent world broods with warm breast and with ah! bright wings."7

The mothering Spirit is once again brooding over creation and stirring its waters. The contemporary ecological movement is spiritual as well as scientific. The connection of body and spirit that is part of the Magdalene moment also comprises a bonding with the earth. The waters stirred by God's breath flow into and through numinous spaces such as the pool of the goddess in Bath, the spaces where mortals can pass into the realm of mystery that is normally veiled from human sight. *Ruach* also blows sparks of compassion and love into the tiny thin places in the human heart, through cracks and vulnerabilities in our self-defences, to allow God's work of creativity to flow up and into the surface of our lives.

A few years ago I spent some time at a friend's cottage on a small island in the Magnetawan River in Ontario. Every day I stood barefoot upon ancient metamorphic rock that still bears the imprint of the molten fire that coursed through the veins of the earth in the age of its formation millions of years ago. For me, this was a daily reminder of the living energy of God that flowed through this rock. Seated by the warm pool of sacred water that is open to the sky in Bath, the holy place of Sul and Minerva deep beneath the green contours of the Mendip Hills, I had reflected on the circles of connection that bind the whole of creation. Standing on the traces of fire within the rocks beside the Magnetawan River, I heard again the soft whoosh of those bright Spirit wings over the waters. The traditional hymn for the feast of Pentecost, *Veni, Sancte Spiritus* — Come, Holy Spirit — invokes the Holy Spirit as the God who gives sweet refreshment in the heat of life's toils and who heals the wounds of creation. Her sweet breath of love touches those whose hearts are rigid or fearful and infuses them with the courage to be more daring. She inflames spirits frozen into indifference or denial with a new passion for justice.

By opening ourselves to the mystical power of the universe, we can once again feel the sacred fire and energy of the cosmos. The arteries of fire in ancient molten rocks of the Magnetawan, like the heat of the goddess' pool in Bath, have continued to reverberate in my imagination like a deep basso continuo in a piece of classical music. As our hearts become attuned to the heart of the universe, we can experience the waves of generativity that flow directly from God.

The earth is now suffering as a result of the enormous harm inflicted on it by humans. Global warming, environmental destruction and species extinction threaten the well-being of animal, plant, river and rock alike. Creation suffers with the elimination of so much beauty, diversity and the individual and interconnected species that have evolved over thousands of years to reach the culmination of their existence. Now they are at risk of extinction within a matter of a few years. Chronic poverty and the ravages of war and disease affect more than half the human race. It is by and large the poorer nations of the earth who are paying the price of the overconsumption of the rich as their resources are seized, their forests are depleted and the effects of pollution engulf their water supply.

Is it possible, in our time, to reinvent the human as a source of joy for the earth and its creatures? Can humans move away from domination to a relationship of partnership with all living beings? We desperately need to invoke the courage of a new Pentecost, that God's *ruach* may touch us anew with tongues of fire, and a mighty wind blow us out of the upper rooms of our denial and fear with new power to heal the earth.

The ominous signs of potential disaster and the confusion of the times we find ourselves in — betwixt and between old certainties and postmodern ambiguity — have led many religious leaders to call for a return to old rules and structures in pursuit of the bygone security of a supreme, transcendent and omnipotent God the Father. But this revival of old-time religion will be ephemeral in the long run because the old structures cannot contain the flow of the new global consciousness.

Creation spirituality, a catch-all term for the "greening" of theology and spirituality, is part of this growing global consciousness. New research into the origins of the universe and the interrelatedness of all planetary life is having an impact beyond the scientific community. The current ecological crisis has a profoundly spiritual dimension.

The Earth Charter was first proposed at the UN's Rio de Janeiro Summit on the Environment. Maurice Strong and Mikhail Gorbachev launched the final stage of drawing up the charter, with the support of the Dutch government, in 1994, and UNESCO approved it in 2000. The Earth Charter Secretariat was formed in 1997 and is now based in Costa Rica. To quote the prologue from the Charter: "We stand at a critical moment in Earth's history, a time when humanity must choose its future. As the world becomes increasingly interdependent and fragile, the future at once holds great peril and great promise. To move forward we must recognize that in the midst of a magnificent diversity of cultures and life forms we are one human family and earth culture and one Earth community with a common destiny."[8]

For centuries, Christian theology has operated under a number of assumptions that have fostered a heedless and often negligent attitude to the earth. First, we have been taught that human life is innately superior to all other life on earth, and that it is the only form of life that really matters. The earth has been viewed as a collection of inanimate objects rather than as a living and changing organic whole. The second, and closely connected, belief is that God has placed humanity in total control of the earth, to have dominion over its resources. Third, Christians have traditionally regarded human existence as transitory and hold that the real purpose of human life will be realized after death, in eternal life with God in heaven. This planet is but a "vale of tears," as an old Catholic prayer to the Virgin Mary, the Hail Holy Queen, describes it, on the journey to our real destination in heaven above.

Changing these attitudes requires a shift of the heart as well as of the head, one that engages emotion as well as reason. We can stare numbly at the statistics that tell us that we are draining the earth's waters and poisoning the earth's air, but unless the heart is open and engaged in love for the earth, the mind and spirit remain locked in a paralysis of apathy or reactionary resistance.

Within the past quarter of a century, the new Religious Right in the United States, a good friend of the corporate interests that benefit from increased consumption and the increased pollution that accompanies it, has moved from indifference to the fate of the earth towards a positive glee at the prospect of its imminent demise. The Right's Christian wing has a highly developed theology to usher in the end of the world. They believe that the destruction of the earth, whether by pollution or nuclear conflict, is to be welcomed because it will serve to hasten the Rapture and the all-out war of Armageddon. According to these Christian pundits, we have already entered the final stages before Armageddon. Apocalyptic conditions of famine and hunger, war and disease stalk the earth. The millions dying of AIDS in Africa are factored into this hateful prophecy. Now that humanity has entered into the last days, the earth will be swallowed up by the great vengeance that God will wreak upon sinners, whom they identify as the "other" — such as people with AIDS, or the undeserving poor — people, in other words, who are not like them.

This is not the first time that economic greed and religious zeal have been close partners in the history of the crimes inflicted on the earth and its peoples. Christian missionaries followed in the wake of military colonization, invoking the name of Christ as a pretext for violent destruction of indigenous cultures and spirituality. They dismissed as primitive, pagan and therefore worthless those aboriginal values and practices that honoured the sacredness of the earth and sought to work in harmony with it by reverencing the divine at work in the seasons and cycles of earth's generous fertility. Communication with animals was celebrated in art, totems and other elements of culture that recognized the essential value of animals to the well-being of humans.

But God did not just disembark in the Americas with the priests who followed in the wake of Christopher Columbus and the conquistadores. God did not initiate communication with humanity only with the call of Abraham and Sara in the biblical era. God had already been actively nurturing the cosmos for millennia. God's work was celebrated in the rituals of indigenous peoples that made earth and its animals holy and its fruits reverenced. Some have argued that missionary Christianity contributed to the onset of secularization by attempting to purge these ancient memories of earth's holiness from human experience, thus stripping the natural world of its intrinsic holiness.[9] The beauty and truth of God is manifested in the contours and complexities of the earth. Science as well as religion has alienated us from cosmic-creative life. Christianity may have downgraded the earth into a mere transient stop, a place where humans were to be tested on the route to the afterlife, but it was science that later characterized the earth as a source of raw materials, a lifeless machine. Earth's delicate internal balance, or autopoesis, was dislodged by the depredations of technology. So as a result of the influence of both religion and science, humanity lost the belief in nature as revelation of the divine and lost sight of the fact that we have co-evolved within the universe for at least 4 billion years.

Judeo-Christian and Islamic religious tradition proclaimed that humanity's relationship to God only began some five thousand years ago. Some believers today still argue that the earth was created only thousands of years ago, despite all the evidence that God has been at work in the universe for some 13 billion years and that humans came into being as a result of our kinship with the rest of creation. But now we are on a homeward pilgrimage to reconnect with the earth by looking back in time before patriarchy and imagining a future beyond it. If we are to take the next step, we must allow the earth as well as the heavens to guide us into an engaged cosmology.

Human survival, as well as that of the planet, will depend on a change of consciousness, on two major shifts in understanding — of ourselves, and of how we relate to the rest of the cosmos — so that we can reincorporate this ancient wisdom. First of all, we must recognize that humanity is an undivided species: our oneness as humans is deeper than our divisions into ethnic, national or racial groupings. And secondly, that we humans are irreversibly and intimately connected to all life on the planet.

More and more people are recognizing that the energy of God moves through structures of mutual relationship, not through hierarchies of domination. Science in our day is becoming the handmaid of mysticism. The new mystical interaction of science and spirituality is one of the exciting elements of Magdalene spirituality. Change is happening through a deep dreaming in human consciousness, which is birthing new understanding and new possibilities into being. The survival of the planet depends on a new sense of justice that is inspired by new dreams and creative imaginings, as humanity assesses the implications of the new cosmology in so many different spheres. Although division and competition have marked the past two millennia, and religion has often played a role in fomenting the rivalries that have led to destructive behaviour, a gigantic shift in awareness is called for — one that will lead humans to think of themselves not as warring factions in competition for limited resources but as one species that belongs to the whole of creation.

A new world is possible. We now know that the universe,

God's great work, is teeming with life and constantly evolving. It began approximately 13 billion years ago with a great burst of energy that blazed out with fearsome intensity. This flaring forth created the stuff out of which the material universe would evolve. Out of this initial elemental mass, the first galaxies emerged a million years later. There were approximately 100 billion galaxies in all, with our own Milky Way but one of them. The primal stars died but as they expired, they exploded into a burst that brought forth our sun. The sun then spun off a web of planets bonded to itself in a reciprocal orbit of life.

Ever since the original flaring forth, a vast stream of energy has connected all the parts of the cosmos. In theological terms, this energy is the life force of the God that imbues the whole of creation with the likeness of God's own being. At the heart of cosmic life lies a fundamental characteristic that is pivotal to understanding the way it functions: every being that has life, from the simplest particle to the most intricate galactic formation, is related and interdependent.

The energy that powers the process of cosmic evolution is a primal relational force of attraction. As Diarmuid Ó Murchú, mystic and ecologist, writes, "For those who believe in God, this energy is a primary characteristic of divine creativity; indeed it might well be the most tangible evidence of God's creativity at work in the cosmos."[10] This is a God who delights in the beauty of even the smallest motion of cellular life and who imbued the material universe with what seems to be a primary relational attraction. The first cells that emerged on earth took millennia to adapt the power of oxygen. Out of this arose more complex cells and the development of meiotic sex. This involves the division of a cell's nucleus in half twice, into four cells with identical genetic material, or chromosomes. In a long process that ultimately evolved into human reproduction through the uniting of sperm and egg, two cells with separate nuclei evolved. These were able to unite without consuming each other in the process, as had happened in the earlier stages. Thus the new cell that emerged possessed blended genetic information. Different cells were created and recreated out of the stored genetic memory in each nucleus. This complex process of relational attachment also produced the earliest forms of life in the sea. Long before the first humans walked the earth, amphibians emerged from the sea to develop the lungs and legs necessary for survival outside the waters of the ocean. And it is to these early creatures that we humans trace our lineage.

Every person who walks the face of the earth carries the imprint of millions of years of evolution. The Genographic Project, a joint enterprise announced by the National Geographic Society and IBM, is designed to chart human development back to its common origins in Africa roughly 150,000 years ago. "Ultimately everyone around the world traces back to a common ancestor," explained the project director, Dr. Spencer Wells.[11] The Genographic Project is mapping the story of human evolution from this common ancestor by comparing DNA samples from different populations all over the world. The project will then trace the migration of early humans by examining the genetic markers present in different groups of indigenous peoples. By tracing migration patterns from the very beginnings of our species to the present day, this project will demonstrate the great diversity of life within the context of a fundamental unity.

The rediscovery of a common human ancestry has the potential to help overcome the competition and prejudice that pits one branch of the human family against another. We are all part of a common humanity. Everyone on earth is genetically related. We are all descended from the original galactic explosion that showered the dust of millions of stars into the expanding universe. As they lived and then died, those stars released the chemical elements necessary for life; we ourselves are made of that matter. As the astronomer and director of the Vatican Observatory, George Coyne, stated in a talk given at the Vatican in August 2005, "There is no other way to have the abundance of carbon necessary to make a toenail than through the thermonuclear processes in stars. We are all literally born of stardust."[12]

The well-being of the human race and of the earth now becomes a common project. Intuition and creative imagination drawn from consciousness of the new cosmology can fuel the innovative ideas that we desperately need to turn around the destructive patterns of competition and conquest. If we are all made from stardust, we carry within us traces of the first thermonuclear galactic explosions. Our bodies are as old as the first elements from which the universe was formed, and as young as the perfectly formed nails on the toes of a newborn baby.

And that baby's exhalation of breath — that first cry that every parent longs to hear — is only possible because our fish ancestors developed lungs.

Through meditation many people come to recognize and receive the currents of God's creative energy that have been flowing through the universe for millions of years. By awakening consciousness to the sacred dimension of the earth, we honour the processes and patterns of the earth's story as a context of sacred revelation. And then prepare to give our lives away, as did the first stars. The only way to find life, says Jesus, is to lose it. The only way to live an abundant life is to give it away.

Our bodies have evolved to reflect the generosity of this inheritance. The generative energy of the stars translates into the mystery at the heart of sex. Two can become one only if they surrender the egocentric desire to use sex for individual self-satisfaction or power. To give life to each other rather than drain it. Procreation is not the only purpose of sex, although the creative energy that results in the conception of a child is undoubtedly one of the most beautiful experiences that a couple can share. Sexual passion generates the energy to look outward, to widen the embrace to include care of the earth or those who are suffering. This is the basis for a holistic spirituality, one that has overcome the body-soul dualism and aligns itself with the deep cosmic thrust of sharing life by giving it away, immersing itself in the struggle for justice for all of earth's creatures. The generativity of the universe can issue into a myriad life forms.

Giving away life in order that another new form may emerge is the second fundamental characteristic of the universe. All the changes that have occurred as the universe evolves have followed a process of dying and rising again. As the first stars were extinguished, they sent forth new clouds of matter that formed into galaxies. Billions of years later in the chain of evolution on earth, several branches of early hominids died out but bequeathed elements to the line that eventually mutated into *Homo sapiens*. So even though the life of any given organism appears to end, it rises again transformed. In theological terms, the transformative action of new life arising out of the death of the old is a process known as *kenosis*.

Kenosis is a Greek word that means "self-emptying." It is an act of self-transcendence that involves giving up a part of one's own individual wants, even to the extent of dying in order that another's life may flourish. In the letter to the Philippians, Paul used the word *kenosis* to describe the love at the heart of the life, teachings and death of Jesus, who emptied himself of divinity, even to the point of death, in order to lift humanity and the cosmos to God.

Long before Jesus walked the earth, the kenotic cycle of self-transcendent love had come into being at the heart of creation. The sun, that great star at the centre of our solar system, gives away its own life every second that it shines. Without the sun, life on our planet would wither and die. But in the process of giving life to the earth, the sun itself is dying. Creation can be described as the primary sacrament, the original paschal mystery of death and resurrection in which each form of life gives of itself to sustain and nourish the others.

No other planet similar to earth, with its delicately balanced ecosystem, exists within our solar system. The earth is a unique planet within a cosmic creation that is ongoing. God has been at work in the universe for some 15 billion years. This new cosmology has vastly expanded our notion of God and of God's activity. A religious understanding that confines the work of God to just the small period of a few thousand years delineated in the Bible is far too limited to accommodate the new knowledge we have acquired of just how magnificent and munificent the universe really is. Just as Aquinas took the paradigm of Aristotelian thought that was revived in Europe and made it into a new synthesis of theology, so the task of the present is to attempt a synthesis of the new cosmology and religious traditions.

The cosmos and the planets within it form an organic whole. The forces at work in the universe evolved not in competition but in relationality. In *The Origin of Species* (1859), Charles Darwin proposed that the progression of evolution was driven by the survival of the fittest. Contemporary theorists often use the term co-evolution to convey a modification of the ruthlessness of Darwin's schema. Evolution is now seen as a more cooperative, interdependent and ongoing process. "Evolution does not take place in the universe; all life co-evolves with the universe."[13]

The universe does not operate in terms of hierarchies of

inclusion and exclusion but as a communion. Each species, each facet of the universe, co-exists in mutual interdependence. Plants, for example, are not a "lower" form of life than animals. The photosynthesis of plants is the vital process that enables the animal and human worlds to exist and function.

The original sin of humans, as recounted in the Book of Genesis, was to turn away from their interdependence with the earth, symbolized by the myth of the expulsion of Adam and Eve from the Garden of Eden.[14] In the second chapter of the Book of Genesis, we are told that God created a garden overflowing with goodness and abundant life. The humans received the earth as a gift from God and were given the stewardship of its resources. So their original identity is to be moulded in the image and likeness of their generous creator. They experience intimacy with each other and kinship with all other forms of life.

But then a choice is presented to them. They can live out their relationship with the creator as stewards of earth's mysteries, replicating the divine impulse to share power with the rest of creation and care for it with respect. Or, as Satan the Deceiver invites them to do, they can grasp at a fool's paradise symbolized by access to the tree of knowledge. The delusion set before them by the tempter is one of superhuman power over creation. Satan invites them to take a step out of the boundaries of stewardship and become proprietors instead. Take the apple by force, tear it off the tree! Take it for yourselves! Satan proclaims that the tree is unworthy of the respect that God has demanded for it. Tempted by the illusion of domination over the fruits of the tree, they began to plunder the earth.

Refusing to emulate the model of a God who walks side by side in companionship with humans in the cool of the evening and sees them naked without shame, Adam and Eve were tempted by the delusion of a God who rules through mastery, fear and guilt. The power to dominate the earth and its peoples will belong to Adam and Eve too, if only they take it by force. Their true relation of humanity and the earth was broken by their choice to dominate rather than work in partnership with creation.

Jesus' parables of gardening, farming and keeping house tap into the wellsprings of our longing to return to a world of relation with the earth. After the crucifixion, Jesus is buried in a garden. In death, he returns to another Eden. On the first Easter Sunday, the women also return to the garden where he has been buried. It is the women who know where to look for the renewal of the earth that will be ushered in by the resurrection. This is a deep truth that has been overlooked in Christianity to date, but the Magdalene Christians of our time will recognize the emerging signs of Christ's presence in the contemporary world.

In the Gospel of John, Mary Magdalene runs to summon Peter and John to the empty tomb, but after they have seen it, they go back to the upper room without understanding what has really taken place. Mary stays behind in the garden. She waits alone, weeping. When she becomes aware of another presence in the garden, she thinks it is the gardener.

How significant that this should be the guise in which she first perceives the Risen Christ. The mystery of Jesus' death and resurrection has recreated that Garden of Eden, where divinity walked with humanity without any barrier between them. The resurrection of Christ brings humanity full circle to a recognition that God walks through creation in the warmth of the early morning sun or the cool of the evening starlight. God is immanent at the centre of creation, at the heart of the delicate and beautiful ecosystems of our planet. Thus, we live and move with God now, as we walk the earth.

Jesus called Mary by name with that special lilt in his voice that she recognized. She responded with an intimate term of endearment that she probably only used privately with him — Rabboni, or "little rabbi." When Jesus and Mary embraced on that Easter morning, Mary was not just touching the hem of Jesus' garment, as the beautiful but ethereal painting by Fra Angelico in the former Dominican Convent of Saint Mark in Florence portrays. This was the embrace of Jesus who "often used to kiss her on the mouth" of the Gospel of Mary. The touch of Jesus and Mary in the garden was redolent with the sensual magnetism of spring.

After that first embrace, Jesus, in John's gospel, said to Mary, "Do not hold on to me because I have not yet returned to the Father."[15] For centuries in Christian tradition, this phrase has often been interpreted to mean that Jesus rebuked Mary for attempting to transgress into the forbidden zone of bodily contact with him. This interpretation arose out of the anti-sexual, dualistic philosophy that has held the church captive for so many centuries. The "Rabboni" term of endearment Mary uses when she recognizes Jesus does not anticipate a dispassionate dismissal of her affection. Jesus' words "Don't hold on to me" are a call to a joint enterprise: to transform the power of the intimate personal gesture into an expansive embrace of all creation by the new life released by His resurrection.

Through their embrace, Mary Magdalene and Jesus restored Eden's promise. They are the new partners in the stewardship of creation, a creation restored to its pristine life by Jesus' resurrection. The full fruits of their embrace are still to be realized in each of us. Magdalene Christianity, inspired by that glorious meeting on the first Easter, is now poised to generate renewed male and female energy. Jesus' resurrection startled the women who recognized and acknowledged its power. We are experiencing a similar disorientation today, as we learn humbly to acknowledge that we are not the centre or measure of all things in the cosmos. Moving from domination over creation to partnership involves both reclaiming our roots and stretching the imagination into a new future. As Ó Murchú writes, "This remembering is unambiguously relational, sexual, erotic and creative."[16] Such is the erotic justice of this Magdalene Moment. Anyone who has experienced the delight of lovemaking in a garden or meadow in the spring, with insects buzzing and the scent of the grass heavy in the air, will have experienced something of the return to Eden promised within that Easter garden. Humans are the only creatures who embrace and make love face to face.

We have the gift of being able to imagine what it must be like to be "the other," to be deeply compassionate by being drawn out of ourselves and entering into the deep mystery of another person. Who can resist the loving smile on the face of the partner and the radiant shine in the eyes of a lover? Through sex, the universe calls us to justice — to seek ways of being more intimate with all creation, to return once again to the Easter Eden.

One new field of study that has opened up the dimensions of the divine presence within creation is the movement known as ecofeminism, which explores the links between the oppression of women and the exploitation of nature. Its starting point is a recognition that the dualistic structure of Greek philosophy inherited by Christianity has influenced cultural assumptions that identify women with the physical body, sexuality, and the earth. Masculinity represents spirit, mind and control of the emotions.

The natural processes of the human body, especially of women's bodies, have sometimes been feared because they are aligned with the processes of nature. The monthly cycle of the moon that draws the great oceans into its gravitational orbit is linked with menstruation, once considered a sacred sign of a woman's participation in the cycle of fertility. But culturally and economically women's lives, and in particular their bodies, have been devalued by association with reproduction, child rearing, food production and cooking — activities that are mainly in the private sphere of the home and devalued in relation to the public sphere, the site of male power and activity.

But at the dawn of human history, the image of the divine

was a fertility goddess, reflecting the fertility of the earth. These goddess religions often linked sex with the sacred. The erotic rites associated with the worship of the goddess were not intended to subject women to dominance by men, but viewed women as a threshold into the divine. Sexual intercourse was a way of communing with the divine and assuring the renewed fertility of the earth. Women's bodies were not considered a source of evil but a gateway into the sacred. The communion of male and female was linked with the fertility of the earth. Ecofeminism is not a single construct but varies in expression according to the context from which it emerges. Broadly speaking, it calls for a deconstruction of the systemic hierarchies that have placed humanity in control of nature, which is envisaged as primitive and in need of domestication, and men in control of women, also seen as inherently sinful. Ecofeminism explores and unmasks the links between these two oppressions. It rejects the separation of the transcendent realm of God from the earth, a separation that projects God "as dwelling only in a superterrestrial realm outside the universe and ruling over it."[17]

The desire to foster a deep connection between women and nature is caught on the horns of a dilemma in that this connection has been used in the past to denigrate women. But precisely because women have been adversely affected by a malevolent association with the earth, they may now be the best able to defend its interests.

In our own time the depredation of the earth is also linked to the exploitation of poor women in the consumer-driven global market. Most of the world's poor are women who survive on subsistence farming, in cultures where women have traditionally worked in the fields. Many of them are now migrating to factories or large-scale agribusinesses in order to pick and pack the flowers and fruits that will grace the tables of more privileged women elsewhere. The smallholdings of the poor in equatorial countries have been transformed into huge berry fields so that we in the northern hemisphere can eat summer fruits in the winter. Driven off their land by the appetites of consumers in wealthy countries, the rural poor often migrate to the edges of the forest and cut down trees to provide fuel for cooking. The great lungs of the planet are thus being slowly destroyed minute by minute by these tiny lacerations.

The solution to this human and ecological disaster lies in a change of appetite and consumption in the north. A preferential option for the earth also benefits poor peoples, the majority of whom are women. "The arc of the universe is long," said Martin Luther King, "and it bends towards justice."[18] It is important that ecological sustainability and social justice not be pitted against each other, although their interconnection is complex. It is easier to practise recycling than to solve the disparities between rich and poor nations that would involve more profound changes to our lifestyle. Unravelling the links between local and global levels of social and environmental oppression is long and arduous work. But it is a deeply spiritual endeavour with many rewards.

Christian sacramental rites preserve a connection with the waters, earth, bread and wine that are the materials of the Eucharist. The sacraments are cosmological rituals.

But how can we celebrate the Eucharist with genetically modified wheat? Or wine with grapes gathered by workers who have not been paid a just wage for their labour? Or baptize our babies with polluted water? It is hard to celebrate a healthy sacramental spirituality on a sick planet. Still, divinity is manifest, especially within the most marginalized peoples of the earth. The identification of the poor with the broken body of Christ is the great gift of the Christian religion to cosmic thought. "Whatsoever you did to the least of these my sisters and brothers, you did it to me."[19] Now the broken body of Christ includes the earth itself as well as its poorest people. Poverty and environmental degradation are linked, and Christ suffers within both.

Our age has its own martyrs, saints who have been killed defending the earth and the poor. Dorothy Stang, an American Sister of Notre Dame de Namur, was murdered on February 12, 2005.[20] She was seventy-three years old and had been in the Amazon for more than forty years. She had confronted the loggers and ranchers responsible for the illegal deforestation of this region. She also spoke out for the rights of the poor, encouraging them in the practices of sustainable farming and organizing them to stand up for their rights to the land.

Dorothy Stang's religious vows of poverty, celibacy and obedience were not lived out in some externally imposed self-mortification. She gave of her life with generosity but at the same time lived frugally herself. She is a role model for a new asceticism and conversion in the rich world, calling us to tread lightly on the earth, to consume less so that all may share its resources. Her death reminded us northern consumers of the extent to which our inordinate appetite for meat implicates us in the death of the forest.

Suffering, death, chaos and destruction, creativity and transformation are integral to existence. We are not only redeemed by Jesus' death and resurrection but placed at a new level of understanding — that God participates in the suffering of the world even as God participated in its creation. The Spirit in Genesis does not eliminate the dark but hovers over it. God does not eliminate chaos but lives in creative tension with it. Raising awareness of the connection between patterns of consumption in rich countries and the destruction of the environment in the southern hemisphere and elsewhere is a most urgent task. Patterns of consumption in rich countries are wreaking havoc on the earth. One strategy, easily pursued at home, that can help to bend the arc of the northern hemisphere closer towards justice is to return to bioregional patterns of shopping and eating. Can Canadians, for example, cease to demand strawberries and mangoes all year round and switch back to buying local crops in colder months if it would help save the planet? This would not only help to restore the environmental balance of global regions, but at the same time alter the patterns of consumption that keep the poor in economic thrall to our needs. Land in Latin America is being converted from producing traditional food crops to producing fruits and flowers for the North American market. A reduction in northern demand might help provide an opening for the land to be returned to its rightful use, to feed the local population, the vast majority of which lives at subsistence level.

Agribusiness in the developed world has swallowed up the smaller farms that used to supply local markets with a variety of agricultural produce. Grown further away from consumers, food is now transported over greater distances. The trucks hauling these loads of food also contribute to air pollution. Our patterns of food consumption carry a hidden cost in the increase in environmental degradation, health problems, the loss of local jobs and markets and a decrease in food self-sufficiency. By the time these negative effects are publicly acknowledged, it may be too late to reverse them.

In the north, the demand for meat has led to intensive livestock farming. Not only are the animals involved kept in cruel conditions, but huge amounts of liquid manure drains into the water supply. Giant feedlots for cattle and hogs overwhelm the ability of local cropland to absorb it all, and the run-off contaminates local water systems, causing disease and even death. This cycle can be broken: it is a matter of choice. We can choose to live in harmony with the natural systems of bioregions if we wish to. Bioregions have soft borders — food and energy and water pass across the borders and cannot be corralled or sold off. The quality of life — even the survival — of future generations will be linked to the willingness of this generation to move towards sustainable living. Do we need more pristinely green golf courses in the world, especially in areas where water is scarce? As consumers we have the power to effect change. For example, consumers can leverage change towards the creation of a more sustainable market through their buying and eating habits.

In *Dark Age Ahead*, visionary Canadian author Jane Jacobs suggests that there are symptoms of cracks in the social fabric of North American culture that, if not attended to, could lead to its eventual demise.[21] She calls these cracks "the five jeopardized pillars": namely, stresses on families and communities; a decline in higher education; the effective price of science and technology; the lowering of taxes and government intervention to address social problems; and the subversion of self-policing by the learned professions.[22] These five symptoms, she believes, are inextricably linked to the wider global problems of environmental degradation and the growing gap between rich and poor. In *Collapse: How Societies Choose to Fail or Succeed*, Jared Diamond lists twelve serious environmental problems facing past and present societies. The first four concern the loss or destruction of natural resources involved in the encroachment of humanity into forest and wetland areas, the depletion of the stock of food obtained from the wild, the loss of plant and animal biodiversity, and the erosion of arable land. The reduction of the world's energy sources, freshwater supply and the photosynthetic energy derived from sunlight form the next three. Diamond then describes the effect of pollution by toxic chemicals, the introduction and spread of non-native plant and animal species, and the generation of atmospheric gases that are harming the ozone layer.

In the final analysis, according to Diamond, the combination of the growth in the world's population and the impact of this growth on the environment poses the greatest threat. This is driven by the natural desire of people in the developing world to attain the living standards of the industrial nations, which they are aware of as a result of the revolution in global communication. A world where everyone was able to attain the same living standards as we do would be unsustainable.[23]

At the heart of this analysis lies a key spiritual question. Can we, particularly those of us who live in privileged societies and who also profess belief in a compassionate God, make the necessary adjustments to downsize our demands on the earth's resources in order to ensure its survival?

In the short term, the suffering of the earth and the poor is likely to increase. The resort to violence to seize the earth's resources, as manifested in the American invasion of Iraq or the incursions of Shell Oil into the tribal lands of the Ogoni in southern Nigeria, which cost Ken Saro-Wiwa his life, will no doubt occur again. But new organizations are springing up in opposition, creative networks that are allowing for progressive dreams for the future.

In 2004, the Nobel Peace Prize was awarded to Wangari Maathai. She is the founder of the Green Belt Movement, a grassroots women's group that has planted more than 30 million trees in Kenya and other African countries. This movement has not only halted the deforestation of this part of Africa, but also empowered thousands of poor women by providing them with jobs and economic independence.

Like Dorothy Stang, Maathai has been persecuted for her convictions. In 1999, as a result of her opposition to Kenyan president Daniel Arap Moi's corruption, she was beaten and arrested when she led a protest against the clearing of a forest near Nairobi to make way for a luxury housing development. She signed her arrest warrant in her own blood, which was flowing from a head wound that she received during the beating.

"In my childhood," she said in the poignant conclusion to her Nobel Prize acceptance speech, "I would visit a stream next to our home to fetch water for my mother. I would drink water straight from the stream. Playing amongst the arrowroot leaves I tried in vain to pick up the strands of frogs' eggs, believing they were beads. But every time I put my fingers under them they would break. Later I saw hundreds of tadpoles: black energetic and wriggling through the clear water against the background of the brown earth. Today," she continued, "over fifty years later, the stream has dried up, women walk long distances for water which is not always clean and children will never know what they have lost. The challenge is to restore the home of the tadpoles and give back to our children a world of beauty and wonder."[24]

Human choices and participation can proceed against all odds and often at great cost, the cost even of life itself, to effect change — even though the odds stacked against it are very high. The Kingdom of God begins here and now. It is among us, as Jesus said. We must live now as if creation was restored to the beautiful garden and the waters of the earth were sacred. In tune with the heart, we must realize our kinship with the least among us as we work to return the earth to a healthy balance, to restore the tadpoles to a clear stream.

Healing waters flow from the depths of the earth. To hear the voice of the waters and of the earth is to hear a voice calling for a fundamental and difficult conversion that reaches deep into the private as well as the political context in which we live, to embrace a life in harmony with the dynamics of the universe.

A Magdalene spirituality that rejoices in the restoration of the Easter garden involves an extension of ethical decision-making to include all life forms. It calls for restraint in the use of natural resources, equitable redistribution of wealth and an acknowledgement of human responsibility in assuring the preservation of the life of all species for future generations.

The lives of Sister Dorothy Stang and Wangari Maathai shall not be in vain. They send out ripples of inspiration to others to carry on the struggle. The positive energy of these and others like them pulls us onwards. When we make the transition to a new level of consciousness after death, we may come to understand fully how this happens. We will not die *out* of the universe but become one with it and experience a new energy. The whole universe is still evolving under the impulse of divine energy. The universe is alive. Christ after the resurrection lived in this new state of consciousness. A great world soul like Gandhi or Gautama the Buddha also lived in this aroused state of awareness.

Exposure to the new cosmology has given me a vision of what happens after death. The universe beyond the range of sight or experience is, for me, no longer dark, cold or empty. It is suffused with billions and billions of galaxies. These myriad galaxies in the starry heavens are at home in the great creative delight of God, whose beauty we glimpse every day if we but have the eyes to see. After death I believe that we will be free to wander at will among the galaxies and imbibe the energy of the stars. We will not be transported out of the universe but rather into a deeper awareness of its vastness and beauty. Our consciousness will no longer be constrained by the limits of finite brains.

One constant element of the near-death experiences that have been recorded by so many people is that the other side is friendly. They become aware of dear ones who have passed over, and also of the overwhelming love of God. After death, as Teilhard de Chardin understood from his mystical grasp of the significance of the Eucharist, we will become aware of the life and love of God, which penetrates into every corner of the cosmos. The cosmic movement of death and resurrection is shared in the here and now and the hereafter. Our gift and responsibility is to reflect on, articulate and celebrate this cosmic liturgy that God has granted us. Entrancement with the wonder of creation is a powerful motivation to resist its depredation. It galvanizes us to reinstate God within earth's garden and to re-member that missing part of the body of sacred truth that is sexed, female and earth-centred.

What kind of God would He be
if He did not hear the
bangles ring on
an ant's
wrist

As they move the earth
in their sweet
dance?

And what kind of God would He be
if a leaf's prayer was not as precious to creation
as the prayer His own son sang
from the glorious depth
of his soul —
for us.

— KABIR, "WHAT KIND OF GOD?"[25]

Chapter 4

MAGDALENE ECONOMICS

IN JANUARY 2004 I decided to escape the Canadian winter. I had recently taken early retirement from teaching, and this was the first time in over thirty years that I had been able to take a winter break. South African artist and theologian Dina Cormack, an old friend and founding member of Women's Ordination South Africa (WOSA), had pressed me to visit Durban for years, and at last I could make the trip.

In Durban, I spent three months volunteering at the Edith Benson Home for Babies, a government orphanage that houses 250 children, from four-month-old infants to teenagers of sixteen. I worked with the youngest. Between fifteen and twenty little ones were in the unit at any one time. All were HIV-positive.

I would arrive each morning at seven, when they were just waking up. My first task was to help feed them. This was no mean feat. One by one they would be deposited, bright-eyed, freshly washed and diapered and very hungry, in the room that served as dining and play area. There were no high chairs and only one baby seat, so those of us who were feeding them would sit in a chair and try to balance a couple of babies on our knees with a toddler or two clinging to our skirts. I felt like a mother bird surrounded by little chicks, their beaks constantly opening, chirping in protest whenever a spoonful of food went to someone else. Breakfast was hot cereal. There were no bibs, so getting the food into their tiny mouths without spilling it on their clothes was a challenge.

After breakfast we would have a rough-and-tumble on the mat. Once they got to know me, the older babies loved to climb all over me. Touch was something they craved. It was as much fun for me as for them. I remember one day when the older children had been taken outside, and I was left alone to care for the babies. I just lay on the mat surrounded by active little bairns who could crawl but not quite walk. One played with my toes, while another was touching my back with a small toy and a third was clinging onto my ear and running his fingers through my hair (my blonde hair fascinated them). All the time they were gurgling and cooing away with delight. For me it felt like a therapeutic massage!

At other times when I was sitting on the play mat, some of the older toddlers would barge into me like small steamrollers and knock me over. One girl, Serena, was built like a wrestler. I would see her coming at me, a wicked glint in her eye, arms poised in front of her and hands clenched, and then shrieking with laughter when I toppled over. A typical toddler, she would throw a tantrum if someone else got to me first as she waddled towards me on her unsteady legs.

A couple of older children arrived at the centre one day and sat silent and listless, their faces long and solemn. They had likely been left to their own devices as their parents got sick and died. Lack of vital early sensory stimulation, as well as hunger, are all too commonly direct outcomes of the AIDS crisis. These factors hinder normal development. The orphanage had a daily program of mental and physical stimulation, and it was not long before the two children started to smile and respond to attention. The staff were very encouraged by these small but significant successes.

Then there was Lindy, aged three. I saw in Lindy the makings of a politician. She revelled in any opportunity to outwit or gain an advantage over me. She tested me constantly to see how far she could go, rushing up behind me and bashing me on the head with a variety of toys when I was sitting on the floor with my back turned to her, busy with other children. An amazingly fast learner, she made connections in a flash and experimented fearlessly with new things. I often took her and Anastasia, another older girl, out for a walk in the fairly spacious grounds around the home. We would touch the trees, the bark and the leaves, and they loved to pick up what was on the ground and play in the dirt. The toys in the orphanage were old and broken, and the swings and slides in the outdoor area were in need of repair. This was not through neglect but simply due to a lack of resources to pay for either labour or materials. But the children loved clambering on the broken swings, and touching the earth, the grass and the trees. One day, one of the tree trunks seemed to move: what we had seen was a small mottled gecko, a kind of chameleon whose body assumes the colours of the tree trunk, or a flower, wherever it alights.

Although the babies appeared outwardly relatively healthy and active, I could hear the congestion rattling in their chests as they breathed. Some had raw patches of skin. Their immune systems were not good. The politics of AIDS relief, a controversial issue in the South African government of Thabo Mbeki, had held up the distribution of anti-retroviral drugs to HIV-positive children. Even with these drugs, most of the children would not survive past the age of twelve. Their bodies were unable to resist the onslaught of even minor ailments. And these mites in the orphanage were the lucky ones. Thousands of babies and children in Africa are dying of starvation today, alone and untended, in terrible conditions, their parents too weak with AIDS themselves to care for them.

Some children were already quite sick and weak when they were admitted to the orphanage, and they spent time in a Special Care unit. One day a little boy less than a year old was brought to the nursery from Special Care. He had full-blown AIDS. The first time I tried to feed him a bottle he screamed and threw himself backward, his stomach distended in pain. He improved for a while, but he would often spend several days at a time in the hospital. I looked at his date of birth hanging on his crib, and saw that we shared the same birthday. He was exactly sixty years younger than I was.

When I got home that day, I sat down and wept for a long time because I knew that, in all likelihood, he would die before I do.

The AIDS situation in South Africa seems overwhelming.[1] Tending to a dozen or so babies for the space of a few weeks was but a drop in the ocean. I felt a fierce tenderness towards these small tykes that I had the privilege to hold so close. For one brief period in their little lives, I had their undivided attention. I tried to fill those moments with as much love as possible, as though somehow they would be able to hold the memory of my strong arms and tender eyes in their minds to draw strength from in the future.

I talked to them, cajoled them and tried to impart my own power so that by some kind of osmosis they would all grow up to be Marys with Brass Knuckles. Each of these babies carries stardust from the primordial supernovas. How precious is the life of each one, however brief, and how tragic it is that so many young Africans will never grow up to reach their full human potential. But I am convinced that the smallest act of resistance and love, by each individual, even under desperate circumstances, can help tilt the balance of the world towards becoming a better place.

While I was working at the orphanage, the media in Durban carried a story about a man whose daughter had recently given birth to a child and then died of AIDS. The grandfather killed his newborn grandson because he felt the baby would be better off dead than living for a few miserable months in agony, only to die of AIDS in the end. Who among us could dare to pass judgment on his action? A whole generation of actual and potential parents is being decimated by the virus, leaving the grandparents as the caregivers in many families. The loss of a whole middle generation of parents and workers is having catastrophic effects in every area of life in parts of Africa. When agricultural workers are so sick that they cannot work, how will Africa's already meagre food supply now be preserved? And what will happen to education when so few teachers remain to take charge of the classrooms?

Before the AIDS pandemic struck, the lives of women and girls in Africa were just starting to improve. Literacy and education, key elements in the empowerment of young women and the alleviation of poverty, were on the rise. But now, women account for more than half the current AIDS cases in sub-Saharan Africa, and among those aged fifteen to twenty-four, the proportion is closer to three-quarters.[2]

The cultural obstacles that stand in the way of containing the virus and ensuring the health and emancipation of women are truly formidable. The caregivers at the orphanage told me that in African culture, men are reluctant to use condoms. They imagine it might inhibit their sexual prowess, and some even consider the use of condoms to be a white sexual practice demeaning to black males. The more extreme believe the conspiracy theory that the widespread promotion of condoms is a white strategy to control the growth of the black population.

The Catholic Church carries far more social and political weight in Africa than in other parts of the world. It could be a major force in the prevention of AIDS: instead, its policies worsen the epidemic. Women in Africa, and indeed in many parts of the world, are in no position to insist on abstinence from sex, which is the Church's sole solution for the prevention of AIDS. The Church has consistently refused to concede that in God's eyes, the value of human life is greater than the preservation of its ban on condoms. There is no doubt that the consequences of this Church teaching are lethal.

Elsewhere in the ecclesiastical arena, though, a new generation of African women theologians stands on the front lines in the struggle against AIDS, poverty and discrimination against women and girls. While I was in Durban, Dina Cormack took me to the University of KwaZulu-Natal for a meeting of the Concerned Circle of African Women Theologians. This continent-wide interdenominational group, which includes both Catholics and Protestants, was started more than twenty years ago by Ghanaian theologian Mercy Amba Oduyoye. Now circles meet all over Africa, including both anglophone and francophone sections. While I was there, a pan-African conference was in the works for 2005 on the topic of "Women, Theology and Health."

I was awed by the strength, humour and determination of these women, who were all either teaching or working towards doctorates in theology. In addition to the South Africans, there were women from Malawi, Madagascar and Kenya who had come to study at the Pietermaritzburg School of Theology. Three presented summaries of their research. Fulata Moyo from Malawi told us about the book she was writing, the fruit of a doctoral thesis, called "Red Beads, White Beads." When I heard the title, I thought it would be about the Catholic devotion of the rosary, where the beads for the ten Hail Marys are white and the one designated for the Our Father is red. How naïve I was.

Her presentation proved to be a foray into Magdalene theology, creating links between women's theological insights and the realities of women's lives. This theology was conceived not in the rarefied celibate culture of the seminary but in the raw and immediate context of women's economic and religious oppression. The focus of Moyo's theological investigation was the vulnerability of women to AIDS and the steps women were taking to empower themselves with the God-given right to combat the spread of the virus.

In Malawi, cultural norms forbid women to discuss sex with their husbands. At the same time, because of various taboos, there is a tradition that when women are menstruating they are not available for sex. They hang a set of red beads in the bedroom to signal to the husband not to approach them and they hang white beads when they are available again. In the meantime, the husband often seeks out other women for sex, even multiple partners, increasing the likelihood that his wife, even though she is faithful to him, will become infected. When he returns to the marital bed, his wife cannot protect herself from infection by asking him to use a condom. If she does, he will accuse her of adultery. In a cunning manoeuvre by the man, he reasons that she is requesting a condom because she must have created the risk of infection by being unfaithful during his absence.

Now this is beginning to change. As a result of the AIDS crisis, married women have started to hang out their red beads for weeks at a time. No white beads are appearing. This shift in practice is leading to more discussion among men and women, an increased awareness of the dangers of promiscuity and the possibility of the use of condoms to halt the spread of infection.

After Fulata Moyo's talk, Isabel Phiri, also from Malawi and a Presbyterian minister, then spoke about her research into African independent Christian churches. These smaller churches have mushroomed as more and more Africans search for alternatives to the hierarchical structure and the whiff of colonialism that still hang around the mainstream churches. She told us about one particular woman who had started a non-denominational Christian church early in the 1990s. In 1999, when the Presbyterian Church decided to ordain women, the leaders of the church contacted her to ask if she would like to present herself as a candidate for ordination. She declined because, she said, the community had already ordained her and that, for her, was adequate validation. The participants asked me to talk about my two books, and Isabel roared with laughter when she heard the title of the first, *Is the Pope Catholic?* She went on to tell us that she had had a dream a few days earlier about being elected pope. In the dream, she had looked down and saw that she was clothed in papal regalia. Her first thought was to wonder not only how her husband would react but what the rest of the world would say to a black woman pope! Ah, but no one knows the mind of God, she realized.

The new flourishing of African women's theology reflects a Magdalene moment of grace that will help to open a new threshold of justice. The work of these women theologians is grounded in the concrete realities of life: AIDS, the inequality of women, racial oppression. Isabel Phiri has written extensively on another impact of the AIDS crisis: that men are seeking out ever-younger women for their sexual satisfaction in the belief that they are less likely to carry HIV. Girls are acquiring the AIDS virus at a younger age and they are getting it from older men: "Babies and older girls are raped at home ... outside the home their peers, teachers, neighbours, church leaders and strangers rape them."[3] In another area of KwaZulu-Natal, I visited with women who were doing research into the feasibility of AIDS prevention in rural areas. We talked with the outreach workers whose role it was to visit AIDS patients in their homes. They spoke of women and men dying on the floors of their huts while nearby, babies lay screaming in anguish, starving with a hunger that their parents could not relieve.

As Stephen Lewis, the United Nations Secretary General's special envoy for HIV/AIDS in Africa, wrote in Race Against Time: "The first aspect [of the AIDS pandemic] is the monumental crisis in food. Whenever I travel to Africa today, it seems as though everyone is hungry ... hungry to the point of starvation ... If you ask almost anyone what they need most, including people suffering from full-blown AIDS, they will not say drugs; they will say food. It's a universal reply."[4]

The desperate indigence wrought by the AIDS epidemic is but one aspect of the economic plight of the majority of South Africans. Since the end of apartheid, South Africa has shared the fate of many sub-Saharan countries shut out of the global market by unfair trade and travel barriers. My brief sojourn in South Africa provided a first-hand experience of the vast and increasing gap between the wealthy of the world and the poorest of its poor. In Canada and other affluent countries, the gap between the one-third rich world and the two-thirds poor world is not visible on a daily basis, although the plight of the homeless who live and sleep on the sidewalks of many Canadian cities reminds us of it locally. In South Africa, by contrast, the boundary between the rich world and the poor world is much more porous and visible. Under apartheid, housing and schools reserved for whites were located in the prime areas, which in Durban meant on the hills overlooking the ocean. Beaches were also restricted, with the whites getting the lion's share of the best oceanfront.

Since the end of apartheid, racial discrimination has been officially discontinued and there is universal access to beaches formerly occupied by whites only. The end of apartheid brought the end of the artificial boundaries between white and black townships in outlying areas, where blacks lived in squalid slums without electricity or other services. But the economic condition of the vast majority of the black community has not greatly improved. Properties in white areas remain priced beyond the reach of most blacks. With the restrictions on blacks living in white areas of South African cities now ended, black squatters have moved from the outlying areas into the downtown, and squatter camps now exist cheek by jowl with the mansions of the wealthy. Turning the corner of many a street in downtown Durban or its suburbs, one suddenly comes upon makeshift shantytowns. People live, cook, bathe and sleep on the sidewalk, in shelters made of cardboard, corrugated iron and rags, cooking over an open fire, and bathing in old oil drums. And this situation is by no means unique to Durban: these sorts of conditions also exist on the streets of many other cities in Africa, Asia and Latin America. South Africa happens to be the place where I observed it first-hand.

Violence to persons and property has escalated dramatically. Homeowners protect their property with an elaborate system of security alarms, guard dogs or personal security guards. Fences bristle with electric or razor wire. Gaining access to a private house can seem like passing into a fortress. Heavy security patrols the tourist areas: the visitors are confined within, the indigent are kept outside the perimeter.

In South Africa, the divisions between haves and have-nots happen to be visible to the naked eye. Physical barriers set up to guard against theft in post-apartheid South African society are emblematic of the great divide in today's global economic system. In the so-called First World of more affluent countries, the barriers between rich and poor are less visible than they are in South Africa, but just as effective. Immigration controls and trade barriers erected against people and goods from poor countries function like barbed-wire fences erected to protect the economic ascendancy of richer nations.

Canada, for example, is situated at some distance from the desperate poverty of Third World cities. But Canada places enormous obstacles in the path of potential immigrants from sub-Saharan Africa. It is virtually impossible for a native-born African resident to obtain even a tourist visa to come to Canada. An unspoken policy of segregation in Canadian consulates in poorer parts of the world functions like an invisible barricade around Canadian ports of entry. Canada has a reputation for being a country that welcomes immigrants and refugees. With an aging population, we need youth and energy, which Africa possesses in abundance, to replace our declining population. But an unspoken economic apartheid prevails in Canada's immigration system, which effectively blocks most African immigration. I have heard participants and speakers from Africa who have been invited to attend conferences in Canada tell of being made to go through a humiliating set of detailed family background checks before being permitted to visit. In many cases they have been refused entry visas with no explanation given. When they do manage to obtain visas, their passports are seized as soon as they board the plane. In the course of several visits to Africa, I have experienced apartheid at transit stops in European airports. Whites exit first, then African passengers are frisked by security before being allowed to disembark from the aircraft. Since the terrorist attacks of September 11, 2001, fear of the stranger has prompted additional curbs on border access from poorer countries to richer ones. Although cheap goods are allowed free passage from Latin America to Canada, people are not.

Since the implementation of the Safe Third Country Agreement with the United States on December 29, 2004, the number of refugees coming to Canada from Latin America has dropped dramatically. As of that date, Canada began to deny asylum to refugees arriving at the border via the U.S., and the U.S. began to do the same for asylum seekers arriving from Canada. Since 9/11, the U.S. government has linked refugees with the threat of terrorism, which has led to a proliferation of security measures at the border and an increase in immigration detention centres in the U.S.[5] Canada's reputation as a welcoming country has been tarnished by revelations of Canadian government cooperation in the racial profiling of Canadian citizens of Middle Eastern origins at the U.S. border.

Canada is a country rich in natural resources, developed largely by the labour of generations of immigrants. Now, many of the descendants of those immigrants have forgotten their origins and exhibit hostility toward newcomers. The Canadian system appears idyllic to the rest of the world. Canada has peace and economic prosperity and, so the prevailing wisdom goes, an open door for immigrants and refugees. But in recent years a myth has been created in the minds of many Canadians: many have come to believe that people mainly want to come here to take advantage of our welfare and national health care systems. Once here, so the story goes, new refugees and immigrants abuse Canada's generosity and openness, living a life of leisure supported by the taxes of hard-working citizens. Add to this the fear, fostered since 9/11, that immigrants from certain nations may be terrorist sympathizers, and you have the building blocks of a wall of mistrust towards newcomers.

Another myth that affects not only immigrants but also native-born Canadians goes like this: ours is a land of opportunity, and everyone who comes here and works hard enough has the opportunity to do well. In previous generations, according to the common wisdom, people who arrived here as immigrants worked hard and made a living for themselves and their families. Now they have financial security, a house, and children in university. What worked for them should work for new immigrants today. If newcomers or anyone else can't get a job, then it is because they're not trying hard enough, and they must lack the work ethic of our ancestors. Developed after the Second World War to prevent another outbreak of either fascism or communism caused by economic desperation, Canadian social supports are under attack today as conservative economists and politicians argue that social services and a bloated health care system put brakes on economic growth. According to this way of thinking, the taxes that support social welfare are too high and what we need are more tax breaks, particularly for the wealthy. Tax breaks have become a political and election mantra of conservatives. The Republicans in the U.S. have succeeded in reducing taxes for the rich to the detriment of social programs. The time-honoured ideal of democracy as a system where a government "of the people, by the people, for the people" uses taxation for the common good to ensure the availability of basic necessities to the greatest possible number of citizens has been superseded by the notion that the role of government is to ensure the least possible constraint on the pursuit of material gain.

We have forgotten that in the eyes of God and by virtue of our genetic coding, we are one humanity. The poor to whom we refuse the support of our taxes, or try to keep out of sight, whether in our cities or beyond our borders, are connected to us by shared history and genetic inheritance. But the lives of the poor of the earth, so precious in the eyes of God, do not weigh equally in the balance with the lives of the rich. If the resources used to keep an army on alert to respond to terrorism were diverted into a war on AIDS and poverty, these could be ended within a decade, thus eliminating one factor that led to the spread of terrorism in the first place.

In much of the affluent world, property is accorded higher value than people. The right to property and the pursuit of wealth have become a dogma of consumer capitalism, often upheld by the Religious Right. The predominant sins named in right-wing Christianity, whether Catholic or Protestant, are the so-called sins of the flesh. Those are the transgressions that cause the greatest separation from God. According to many members of the hierarchy of the Catholic Church, homosexual unions and abortion are now grounds for automatic excommunication, and public support for them is now a reason to deny communion to politicians. Whereas waging war to control global resources, cutting back on universal health care, and polluting the environment are not considered sinful.

The focus on individual, personal sexual sin complements the notion of salvation as an individual rather than a collective concern. In right-wing churches, salvation is not social. It is a matter of accepting the Jesus as your "personal Saviour," who will meet all your needs but never challenge your economic or social values. Thus individualistic religion, politics and economics have served and continue to serve one another well. Together, they have now created a view of human nature and its relationship to God and the earth that assures everyone that the operation of self-interest will produce the best possible system. The emphasis on redemption or salvation from sin has all but erased the theology of the sacredness of creation, and social solidarity with the marginalized, from Christian consciousness.

A dogmatic belief in the infallible power of an unregulated market to create prosperity has captured the upper echelons of corporations and governments. Proponents of this doctrinaire market fundamentalism refuse to recognize the lesson of experience — that unless individual self-interest is mitigated by some kind of social constraint, it devolves into destructive individual greed. A Christian spirituality that neglects the notion of economic morality has lost sight of the central teachings of Jesus. The economic practices of Jesus and the first Christian communities provide ample precedent for new and creative configurations for finance and investment. Mary Magdalene was both leader and role model in the early Christian economic project. Along with Joanna, the wife of Herod's steward, and a woman named Susanna and other unnamed women, she was part of the group of disciples who travelled with Jesus. They set out on this journey with no road map to guide them.

While Jesus was alive, some who were drawn to his teaching and by his healing started to live in a different manner. Jesus called his new economic, social and spiritual lifestyle "entering into the Reign of God." Previously, the Reign of God had been imagined as something violent and apocalyptic that was going to arrive at a future date. Jesus said it should start in the here and now. And it did. Right then and there.

Putting Jesus in charge of their lives meant that his original followers made major changes in the way they organized their finances. Luke tells us that the women who travelled with Jesus used their own money to assist him and the other disciples. "Some time later Jesus travelled through towns and villages preaching the good news about the Kingdom of God. The twelve disciples went with him and so did some women who had been healed of evil spirits and diseases: Mary who was called Magdalene from whom seven demons had been cast out; Joanna, whose husband Chusa was an officer in Herod's court; and Susanna, and many other women who used their own resources to help Jesus and his disciples."[6] It is instructive to analyze this small nugget of information.

First of all, Mary of Magdala and the "many other women" were socially and financially independent. Not only were they travelling without husbands or other male partners, but they also had control of and access to their financial resources. Their presence alongside the male disciples was not contingent on the approval of husbands or fathers. Only Joanna is named as a wife, but her husband is not part of the group. It's possible that Mary may have had a small business back in her hometown of Magdala, which was a prosperous fishing port on the shore of the Lake of Galilee.

The other significant fact is that these independent women chose to pool their financial resources and place them at the service of the community. Mary of Magdala, Joanna, Susanna and the other women understood very early that following Jesus requires turning over one's material wealth for the common good. Mary Magdalene and the other women became role models for the early Christian church. Their economic ethic foreshadowed what was to become a key component of the Christian discipleship.

This sharing of wealth initiated by the women became a basic tenet of Christian discipleship. It was adopted by the early Christian community and became a *sine qua non* of reception into the early church. So the economics of sharing wealth, initiated by the women, formed a template for the structure of the Christian community.

The second chapter of the Acts of the Apostles — the same chapter that describes the outpouring of the Spirit on the day of Pentecost — tells us that "All the believers shared in close community with each other and shared their belongings with one another. They would sell their property and possessions and distribute the money among all according to what each one needed."[7] The Spirit of God filled all believers with the same insight that the women had caught on to earlier:

that the first and foremost outcome of baptism for Christians is to share their wealth.

Shortly afterward in Acts, the significance of this tenet is dramatically reinforced. At the end of Chapter 4 we learn that "The group of believers were one in mind and heart. None of them said that any of their belongings were their own, but they all shared with one another everything they had ... There was no one in the group who was in need. Those who owned fields or houses would sell them, bring the money received from the sale and hand it over to the apostles; and the money was distributed according to the needs of the people."[8] The renunciation of material assets is mentioned twice within four chapters: a major emphasis on this particular element of Christian discipleship. But there's more to come.

Early in Acts, in Chapter 5, a married couple named Ananias and Sapphira come onto the scene. They sold some property that belonged to them in order to contribute to the common fund, but "with his wife's agreement he [Ananias] kept part of the money for himself and turned the rest over to the apostles."[9] On hearing about this, the apostle Peter gives Ananias one of the strongest rebukes in the whole of scripture: "You let Satan take possession of you, and you lied to the Holy Spirit."[10]

Peter knew first-hand the sting of that particular rebuke. While still alive and walking along the road in Galilee with his inner circle of followers, Jesus had talked about his trial and death. Peter straightaway remonstrated with him: "God forbid, Lord! That must never happen to you!" Jesus turns on Peter, and you can almost hear him shouting as he responds,

"Get away from me Satan! You are an obstacle in my way, and these thoughts of yours do not come from God but from your human nature."[11]

But now Peter is about to teach the community a lesson it is unlikely to forget. He accuses Ananias of lying to God, whereupon Ananias falls down dead. This is an extraordinary consequence and one of unprecedented severity, given that Ananias had donated the greater part of his holdings to the community and withheld only a part. He had been far more generous than the rich man who came to Jesus and asked what he should do in order to follow him, and was told that he must go sell all he had and give the money to the poor. When this man turned away in sadness because he could not bring himself to do that, Jesus remarked to the disciples: "How hard it will be for a rich person to enter the Kingdom of God!"[12]

Prostitutes, drunkards and all kinds of people of ill repute were welcomed into Jesus' new community. But possessing an excess of money was irreconcilable with acknowledging the Reign of God.

Three hours after Ananias has met with his fate, his wife Sapphira arrives at the place where the community is gathered. Unbeknownst to her, her husband's body has already been removed and buried. So she is still brazen in her lie to Peter: "Ananias," she tells him, "gave you the full amount we received for our property." Before she can take another breath, Peter launches into another tirade: "Why did you and your husband decide to put the Lord's Spirit to the test?" he fumes.

"The men who buried your husband are at the door right now and they will carry you out too!" At once she falls down at his feet and dies.[13] In the next sentence, we are told that "The whole church and all the others who heard about this were terrified."[14] As well they might be. This teaching on the negative impact of withholding wealth from the common good is one the most dramatic in the New Testament. It was meant to send an unequivocal message to the Christian community: failure to observe this teaching carries direct and dire consequences. The story of Ananias and Sapphira shows that those who hoard wealth are unwelcome among Christians. Yet today this teaching on wealth is all but ignored, in both theory and in practice.

I cannot recall ever hearing a sermon preached on Ananias and Sapphira. It's just not something people want to talk about in today's church, this idea of sharing wealth. It's a taboo subject for many congregations. It might upset people too much. Some of the faithful might start thinking that the preacher is a communist. In the minds of some contemporary Christians, that would place a person on the slippery slope to perdition. There are plenty of sermons on charity. That usually implies giving a small percentage of one's income, and any sizeable donation is made with tax deductions in mind. There are groups of Christians who have opted for the more demanding practice of tithing, which means giving away 10 percent of your income to the church or the poor, but in general, charity is not something that detracts from home ownership or the security of investments.

I have studied and prayed over the Gospels and the Book of Acts all my life because they're key sources of my Christian faith. There's almost no mention of the dangers of sex, whether it's sanctioned by marriage, straight or gay. But there's a lot — a whole lot — about the dangers of wealth. No teaching on sex carries the threat of death. Abstinence from wealth appears to be a much more urgent requirement than abstinence from sex, and judgement of riches far harsher than judgement of sex. This is not to argue that sexual morality is of no consequence, or that it should be treated lightly. But there is a need to redress the current imbalance between sexual and social morality.

In theological terms, one of the most glaring sins today is the denial of the link between our lifestyles and the desperate plight of the poor and the degradation of the planet. If a majority of Christians in affluent countries were to adopt a Magdalene approach to economics and place their wealth at the service of the wider community of humanity and the earth, it could lead to an astonishing reversal of the current downward spiral.

Today's version of international capitalism is making those who are already rich vastly richer while leaving the rest of the world's population behind. The increasing proliferation of tax breaks means that wealth is trickling up, not down. Patterns of investment and the flow of money exacerbate this. Before 1970, 90 percent of all international financial transactions were accounted for by trade and only 10 percent by capital flow. Now the ratio has been reversed, with 20 percent of international transactions accounted for by often highly volatile transfers of finance capital not directly related to goods and services. The goal of investment is to extract maximum profit for shareholders, and this, rather than the well-being of workers and the opportunity to contribute to the common good, is what is now driving the global market.

A key theory of the system of free market economics is that the market is self-regulating. Accordingly, rich and poor countries should eventually reach similar levels of per-capita income. For this to work, investment should flow from rich countries, whose citizens possess superfluous capital, to poor countries, where capital is scarce. According to the theory of a free market, the Gross Domestic Product (GDP) should grow at a faster rate in poor countries than in high-income countries, so over time the incomes of the poor will reach a level of parity with the incomes of the rich.

But the gap in income between rich and poor is widening, not converging as the theory insists it should. Over a billion people now live on less than a dollar a day, while at the other end there are now almost 600 billionaires whose combined income adds up to the equivalent of one-fifth of the total economic output of the United States.[15] One of the results of this is that the middle class is disappearing. In Canada, for example, property ownership, which was formerly an aspiration of the majority of those who had a job, is now becoming so expensive as to edge beyond the grasp of even dual-income families.

The notion that the market adjusts itself internally to the cycle of desire and satisfaction, so that the prosperity it generates trickles down to raise the level for all rather than just a few, has in practice proved to be a dismal failure. Adam Smith, the author of the seminal text of capitalism, *The Wealth of Nations*, argued that a graduated income tax would be a means of protecting the security of private property. In his view, if workers enjoyed basic education, health care and good working conditions they would have a stake in preserving stability, the best condition for economic growth. Now, more than two hundred years after Smith wrote *The Wealth of Nations*, the notion of any common interest between workers and investors has all but disappeared, and I wonder if he would have been so optimistic about the outcome of his theory.

Consumerism operates on an ethic of envy and the creation of desires that can never be satiated. The creation of insatiable desire and the fear of loss is part of the modern mythology that drives the market. Consumption is always relative to what others have, and our economy rests on the fulfillment of the wants it arouses in order to maintain itself. The creation of desire is the product of advertising. Advertising creates an addiction to consumption by creating dissatisfaction with what we presently possess. The psychological power of greed projected through advertising is prodigious. Advertising bombards us with invitations on TV and radio, on billboards, in newspapers and subways and on the internet, to participate in a mythical good life where the proliferation of new things will never end. This is coupled with the illusion that these products will satisfy the deep desires of our hearts and that they can be had at no cost beyond the money we spend to buy them.

We start to believe that there is no alternative to the immediate satisfaction of material needs. Our possessions begin to
define our identity and make a constitutive statement about
who we are. We can drink a Coke and pretend that we belong
to a worldwide community of like-minded people who are
all having fun. A new SUV brings with it the illusion that we
are hitting the trail in search of adventure in the wilderness
instead of driving down a suburban street. Any alternative to
this constant craving is avoided, because within it stalks the
fear of losing the ability to consume. This fear serves the purposes of those who hold the reins of economic power. We are
bombarded with the message that if we don't keep shopping,
we are in danger of losing out on the good life. Continual
advertising for the latest products drives the supply side
of production. Fear of the breakdown of this magic circle
creates even more frenetic demand.

The booming economy that is driving this cycle of fear of
diminishment cloaks itself in the vestiges of the "good life."
We are told that we deserve everything we can get. The politics of selfishness fuels the drive for more tax breaks as people
come to believe that the taxes they are paying are too high
and that they are entitled to retain more of their income for
consumer spending. The whole ethos of tax breaks has taken
over people's minds like a kind of political cult. It has brought
with it a significant change in the language of public discourse
in general, and politics in particular. One hardly ever hears
the term "citizens" used to describe voters, or the public in
general. Politicians now refer to voters as either "consumers"

or "taxpayers" — both exclusively economic terms — but rarely as citizens.

In order to protect taxpayers — no longer "citizens" in the market-driven definition of democracy — from the repercussions of their tax breaks, the poor are kept out of sight. They are often prevented by security from entering shopping malls, because they remind people that they too might fall on bad times one day and not be able to shop any more. Seeing the poor is a reminder of the ephemeral nature of material possessions. They must not be allowed too close for comfort, especially where people are shopping and keeping the economic cycle of progress in motion. Increasingly afraid of one another, we also build walls around new housing subdivisions to keep the poor out of our neighbourhoods, which we have begun to call "gated communities."

The same ethos is at work in the deployment of massive security around the G-8 economic summits, part of which is to prevent the delegates from encountering protestors at close range. The politicians and economists must preserve the myth, at least among themselves, that what they are doing is benefiting the global community, that they are basically good people and that they know best how to run the economy. But in fact they are fenced in by the fear that many of their own people are waking up to the fact that they are becoming worse off, not better off, as a result of the current economic system.

Fear of the future is a not unreasonable reaction to the current state of the global economy. We are trapped in a perpetual growth machine, but continuous growth is simply not sustainable. The depletion of the earth's resources, particularly the energy sources dependent on fossil fuels, is accelerating as a result of increasing consumer demand and population growth, as countries such as China and India expand their industrialization exponentially.

Richard Heinberg, whose monthly *MuseLetter*[16] is on *Utne Reader*'s list of Best Alternative Newsletters, is an award-winning writer on sustainable economics and cultural change. In *Powerdown,* published in 2004, Heinberg lists several colliding factors that he and others believe may lead to the collapse of industrial civilization within the next hundred years. Resource depletion, especially of fossil fuels and fresh water, is already evident to many. Continued population growth combined with a declining level of food production is unsustainable. The era of relatively stable climate appears to be ending, as a result of the effect of greenhouse gases and the melting of the polar ice caps. Heinberg also includes the unsustainable levels of U.S. debt, which may lead to a break-down in the operation of financial markets and international political instability. These problems are related to one another in mutually reinforcing patterns.

Access to natural resources such as oil, which are essential to a consumer economy, will be defended by an increasing use of military force. The U.S.-led invasion of Iraq against the consensus of world opinion is a case in point. The Project for the New American Century, the name given to the plan for an American world empire sustained by overwhelming military force, was launched by advisers to George W. Bush during his first term of office. It opens the way for pre-emptive military action to protect and secure American and, by extension, G-8 economic interests.

The current economic cycle of ever-increasing growth in production and consumption also requires an unimpeded depletion of the earth's resources. Economic calculations do not factor in the sustainability of creation. The "earth deficit" that is taking place as a result of the degradation of non-renewable resources is barely discussed in current economic theory. The natural world is still viewed as inanimate and inchoate, a meek and unresisting source of wealth to be mined for human consumption. The accelerating rate of environmental degradation and the loss of resources will affect everyone. The planet's basic functions may be so negatively affected that they will eventually close down. The dwindling of fresh water and the decline of breathable air are only the beginning: it may take more dire effects to wake people out of their denial of the environmental impact of constant consumer gratification.

Heinberg argues that if the United States continues its current policies, then the inevitable competition for dwindling resources to sustain its economy will result in an increase in military invasions to commandeer those of other nations. The only alternative to this is to "power down," as Heinberg calls it: to undertake a worldwide effort toward self-limitation that would involve a reduction in both consumption and population levels. This could be achieved only through a high level of international cooperation, which seems an unlikely prospect. But "powering down" is exactly what was demanded of the first Christians.

For those who recognize our current predicament, looking at the statistics can induce a state of numbness and help-lessness. Heinberg calls this "waiting for a magic elixir":[17] waiting for a global solution that will solve everything rather than trying to make changes now in our individual lives. How can individuals hope to affect the working of such a gigantic and complex economic system? Even when we know that our lifestyle is directly linked to the suffering of other human beings and the potential destruction of the natural world, we lack the will to embark on the road to changing it.

A variety of secular spiritual movements offer the hope of renewal through inner fulfillment. They usually centre on physical and mental health, self-enhancement, and stress management. There is nothing inherently wrong with any of these goals, except that when any or all of them become the entire focus of spiritual life, then the vital element of social solidarity is missed, not to mention any sense of the divine. Spirituality becomes just another commodity to be sampled and consumed. It lacks social commitment and functions like an anodyne, offering the individual an escape from stress but without addressing the systemic factors that cause stress in the first place.

Mainstream Christianity appears to be captive to consumer ideology. Incapable of providing a role model of divestment and economic conversion, churches are cocooned within the security they themselves derive from endowments of property, land and investments. These churches have become deeply embedded within the current economic system. Over the centuries, they have accumulated an extraordinary amount of real estate, art treasures and investments now held in trust, so they argue, for future generations. Their real estate, investments, landholdings and tax privileges have muffled any serious critique of the systemic cycle of wealth and poverty from which they themselves are beneficiaries. Exhortations on the dangers of wealth are usually directed towards others, never against themselves. It is futile to wait for them to lead the kind of divestment, the powering down that is called for in response to the current predicament of the planet and its poor.

Leadership for this is not going to come from the top down but from the bottom up. Grassroots organizations — small groups of engaged but diverse individuals — are beginning to interpret present economic conditions in the light of an ethic of solidarity with the planet and with the poor. This calls for a revival in the human, and especially the religious, imagination. Chapter 3 explored our new understanding of cosmology and creation, a vision of solidarity and interdependence with nature that can arouse the necessary compassion to stave off ecological disaster. We need a similar vision for economic solidarity. We must link the streets and the stars, the new cosmology and the plight of the poor.

We have allowed an economic theory of maximizing profits, regardless of the cost to the environment and the poor, to dictate who we are. We have allowed ourselves to

take on false identities as consumers and taxpayers, no longer
children of God and co-creators of beauty and joy in the cosmos. It is imperative that we set out on the path to recovering
our relational roots. One step at a time is the only way to do
it, and if we all take these small steps then collectively we will
have an impact. In the face of the gaping inequity in the way
wealth is distributed, and the complexities of market globalization, the temptation is to fall back into apathy and denial.
But resistance is possible and necessary, even though it will
take a radical transformation of mind and soul to overcome
the economic and ecological malaise that lies at the heart of
the current global market system. Religious groups across the
spectrum of not only Christianity but other world religions
are an untapped resource in this regard.

Long before the time of Jesus and Acts of the Apostles,
the biblical story of manna, food provided by God for the
Israelites as they wandered through the desert, speaks to the
communal call for the rich to downsize the level of consumption. The bread raining from heaven was sufficient for the
needs of all.[18] There was no surplus and no shortage. Symbol
of the generosity of God, manna was distributed equally to
all, and it could not be accumulated in barns or sold for
profit. God's intention is for the fruits of creation to be
shared. God invited Adam and Eve to be stewards, not plun-
derers, of earth's resources. When they snatched the apple
from the tree, they chose the route of acquisitive greed and
exploitation. The ideal of self-restraint is one of the most
difficult to achieve in a modern consumerist culture, and one

of the most neglected elements in Christian life today.

Jesus showed us a way to break that cycle of proprietary greed. He formed a community where people were expected to commit to the common good and to produce once more God's sustainable and generous harvest. Commitment to Christianity is incompatible with the values that govern the cycle of economic exploitation, competition and greed. The abundant life, according to Jesus and the women in his circle, is not one of endless competition and success in material pursuits. An abundant life is promised when all share the wealth. Jesus' ministry was centred around a table where all were sustained, all shared. The heart of Christian life, the Eucharist, is the unconditional love of God experienced as a gift for all, not as a reward or favour to a few.

Mary of Magdala and the other women enabled the first communities of Christian discipleship to come into being by pooling their resources. Unlike Judas, the keeper of the purse, who begrudged the profligacy of the gift of that other woman who poured a whole jar of precious oil to anoint the head of Jesus, they did not keep count or judge the worthiness of those who gave and partook at the common table. Thus Mary Magdalene worked in partnership with Jesus to maintain the open table, shared for the common good. A Magdalene moment today can derive inspiration from their mutual vision.

The first Christians understood that baptism plunged them into a new life where sustainable economics was not just a visionary dream but a daily reality and the most powerful witness to their faith. Salvation for them began not as the result of some apocalyptic battle at the end of time, but day by day, whenever God's spirit nudged them to be more compassionate and more open-handed with possessions. They lived in small communities on the margins of a great empire alongside others who were also on the fringes of power. The problems of income disparity on an individual and an international level are vast but not insurmountable. There are ways by which we can connect faith and spirituality with our immersion in the marketplace. We too can adopt Mary Magdalene's economic vision based on the redistribution of wealth both for the sustenance of all the world's peoples and for the sustainability of creation.

Theologian Ched Myers refers to this as practising Sabbath Economics.[19] Myers invites communities of faith in the First World to return to the earliest traditions of Christianity and place the observance of economic redistribution at the centre of their Christian discipleship. These teachings are based on a renewal of the Jubilee tradition as described in Exodus, Leviticus and Deuteronomy and developed in the writings of the Hebrew prophets; this tradition was developed and practised by Jesus and the early Christian community. These writings call upon us to reverence God's creation, which yields an abundance of goods for all, provided that humans restrain their appetite for unfettered consumption and learn to live within the limits of sustainability, to use modern terminology to describe an ancient precept. As Myers says: "The world as created by God is abundant and enough for everyone — provided that human communities restrain their appetites and live within limits. Disparities in wealth are not natural but the result of human sin, and must be mitigated within the community of faith through the regular practice of redistribution. The prophetic message calls people to practice redistribution and is thus characterized as 'good news' to the poor."[20]

The biblical requirement of Sabbath rest, and an injunction to let the land lie fallow every seven years, together with the observance of the Great Jubilee every fifty years, inserted a rhythm of rest into the cycle of human labour. In the year of a Great Jubilee, which followed the year of seven times seven, or forty-ninth year, all cultivation ceased. Slaves were to be freed to return to their families, and land that had been sold would revert to its original owner. These practices served to remind people that land was held in trust from God and that they should be grateful for its bounty. Every seventh year people were also freed from unpaid debts. There were general prohibitions against charging interest on loans and on profiting from food sold to the poor. If a labourer became unfit for work, he was still to be paid his wages, and he and his family were to remain in their house. This practice safeguarded against the development of an indigent class of the sick and homeless. These precepts served to remind the Israelites that they were but stewards of the earth, not its owners. The earth belongs to God, the Creator, and the poor have an intrinsic right to share in its bounty.

Jesus was steeped in this Jubilee tradition. For his first public appearance in the synagogue at his hometown of Nazareth, he chose a reading from the prophet Isaiah that echoes the great proclamation of Jubilee: "The Spirit of the Lord is upon me because God has chosen me to bring good news to the poor, to proclaim liberty to captives and recovery of sight to the blind, to set free the oppressed and to announce that the time has come when the Lord will save his people."[21] The passage in Isaiah 61 from which these words are drawn is itself an echo of the Book of Leviticus. As host, Jesus set a table that was frequented by those marginalized by contravention of religious rules and lack of economic status. In so doing, he mirrored the God who sets a table of creation where all may share and be fed.

The enormous disparities in wealth and power that have come to be accepted as an outcome of market forces in today's world were not intended by God but are the result of deliberate human choices. Communities of faith are one arena where economic inequality and ecological depredation can be addressed as moral issues. Churches and religious groups should be discussing personal economics as a key component of fidelity to the gospel. The good news to the poor that lies at the heart of Jesus' message is not just a theory about giving alms but a call to live it out in concrete economic practices of redistribution.

Socially Responsible Investing (SRI) is one way that we can divert resources toward the redress of poverty and pollution. This can be on an individual as well as a corporate level. SRI involves selecting investment targets based on sustainability and social responsibility and raising questions as to, for example, whether or not a company operates in countries where human rights are transgressed, whether it utilizes child labour, whether it offers a just wage and benefits to employees or how it uses natural resources or disposes of toxic waste. SRI and shareholder activism have already made significant inroads into corporate practices, but the potential is still largely untapped. Patterns of consumption, savings and investments can alter the direction of the market. We can make changes both locally and internationally by using the very power of the consumer system to change it from within. There are many concrete ways that consumer denial and indifference can be converted into consumer power. The economic system can only run with the consent of the citizens who buy into it. What we wear, what we eat and what products we use in our homes: all these choices can either support or challenge the current economic cycle. If enough people refuse to buy clothes made in sweatshops, for example, then labour practices will have to change. In 2006, a group of high-school students put pressure on the Toronto Catholic School Board to launch an investigation into the working conditions of those who were making their uniforms and to insist that suppliers ameliorate these if they were found to be harmful to the health of workers, or if the workers were not paid a living wage.

Another example is the idea known as the "100 Mile Diet," which is catching on in Canada and the United States. Two Vancouver journalists, Alisa Smith and James MacKinnon, are writing a book about it, and others such as the Locavores, a group of four women living in San Francisco, are promoting the practice. The challenge is to draw a circle with a hundred-mile radius from where you live and then eat only from within that "foodshed." This is a very practical way to promote sustainability, with ramifications that could transform the global food market.[22]

Foodshed eating in North America could be a form of Magdalene economics whereby inequitable distribution of the world table can be adjusted and the scales of the global market tilted towards justice. In poorer southern countries the fields that have been converted to cultivate strawberries for export to northern markets in winter could be restored to growing a variety of foods suitable for local consumption. Foodshed eating would lessen the costs of transportation, cutting down on the use of fossil fuels and reducing pollution. Local, smaller farmers and sustainable businesses will also benefit from this shift.

We can practise a Magdalene spirituality as we sit down to eat every day. How far did the food we eat travel to get from the farm to the table? Who is present at our table? How inclusive are our households and the values promoted in our homes? Who grows the food we eat and how? Who prepares the meals in the home, and how are they treated? And how does the food we eat reflect justice and harmony with the earth and its creatures? Can we restore a stronger connection to the land and the seasons by choosing to eat food that is produced locally?

If enough of us ask ourselves whether the earth became more toxic as a result of the way we eat or operate our own households, then the producers of toxic chemicals would be forced to change or desist. We know we can effect paradigm shifts in public attitudes. Even a small number of committed individuals can effect societal change. Consider, for example, the campaigns to raise public awareness of the deleterious effects of second-hand smoke. People used to smoke everywhere without restraint — in the house, at the office, in the subway, in movie theatres and in restaurants. The change in attitude toward smoking, and the relatively recent banning of smoking in public areas, have involved an intrusion into the individual freedoms so highly valued by the ethos of consumerism, and the concurrent restrictions on advertising have led to a loss of revenue for tobacco companies. Yet a general consensus over the dangers of even second-hand smoke was enough to cause a change in practice. The same shift in public attitudes could happen with regard to environmental sustainability and trade rules that discriminate against poor countries. Many individuals and groups today are engaged in new ways of living together cooperatively, of responsible investing, and of general downward mobility in material wants.

In his book, Heinberg calls for us to confront the crisis that will result from possible global economic meltdown within a few decades by building what he refers to as lifeboats: local networks of community solidarity that would be as self-sufficient as possible in the event that the infrastructure of society is eroded to the point of dysfunction. Interestingly enough, he refers to these communities as "the new monks."[23] This is perhaps because ideals of communal support and mutual sustenance are deeply embedded within the traditions of Christianity. Yet it is the nations that have the largest Christian populations that are at the top of the table of greed and conspicuous consumption and that have the greatest capital investments in the multinational companies that control the new global economic empire.

Fear of imminent disaster may force us to change our economics, but this is a negative rather than a positive motivation. I would prefer to spread a fire in the imagination that a new world is possible. As Gandhi once remarked, "We must be the change we seek to create." The Magdalene movement that grew out of the ideals of the women who travelled with Jesus provided a role model for bringing about deep change in people's lives in the early Christianity community. Both within and beyond Christianity today, another such Magdalene moment is possible.

We are at
The Nile's end.

We are carrying particles
From every continent, creature and age.

It has been raining on the plains
Of our vision for millions of years.

And our senses
Are so muddy compared to Yours — dear God.

But I only hear these words from You
Where we are all trying to embrace
The Clear Sky-Ocean

"Dear One, come.

Please
My dear ones,
Come."

— FROM HAFIZ, "PLEASE"[24]

Chapter 5

MAGDALENE CHRISTIANITY

IT IS A WARM summer evening in Toronto, and I am sitting in the round bandshell on the edge of Lake Ontario with about a thousand other people. Senegalese artist Youssou N'Dour is playing, and the audience is stomping, swaying and even ululating to the African fusion beat. Tall ships glide silently on the waters behind us, their triangular masts illuminated like pyramids of celebratory candles. The turquoise remnant of the sinking sun has given way to a dark, musky night. Apartment buildings and offices on the city's shoreline are lit up like the torsos of giants. Only a few of the brightest stars are visible.

Toronto. At times like this, I know that despite all the challenges of life in one of the most ethnically diverse cities in the world, the place does actually work. And it must continue to work. The future of the world depends in part on the survival and sustainability of cities such as Toronto.

The continuing success of Toronto and other cities like it will require a concerted effort on the part of individuals, government and corporate interests. Modern metropolises require visionary planners who can inspire the effort needed to accommodate those on the margins. This same creative energy must also be focused on conservation to minimize the drain of large cities on natural resources and on the surrounding environment.

Harbourfront in summer represents the essence of the Canada that I have chosen as my adopted country. I am a first-generation Canadian, a late immigrant to the amazing phenomenon that is Canada. Over the thirty-odd years that I have now lived here, I have fallen deeply in love with this country. Wherever I travel in the world, I always miss both the comfort of cosmopolitan Canada and the vastness of its continental expanse. I breathe a sigh of relief when I return to the safe and generous security of its extensive borders and the multicultural mosaic that is my home city of Toronto.

Historically, Canadian identity has been tentative and evolving, tempered by a respect engendered by the exigencies of living within a sometimes perilous natural habitat, and the cautious humility exacted by the weather: the extremes of a polar winter and a sweltering summer in the south. The great original sin that still casts a deep shadow over Canada's history and its present is the treatment of aboriginal peoples. The combination of the original land grab followed by state-sanctioned religious abuse has caused deep wounds in the fabric of Canadian society that still call for healing.

Canada's modern development has fostered openness to diversity. From the outset of the colonial era Canada's constitutional development has been rooted in the linguistic duality of French and English, enshrined in the Quebec Act of 1774, and religious pluralism, as protected in the British North America Act of 1867. Canada has never had an established state religion. Canadian national culture has been one of compromise, and the national character defies stereotypes. Instead, there has been a history of progressive movement toward the acceptance of pluralism.

As a player on the current global stage, Canada provides a particularly welcoming environment for the emergence of a Magdalene moment. In his book *Fire and Ice*, Michael Adams, president of Environics Research Group, examines the differences between Canada and the United States. Adams argues persuasively that while economically the two countries are closely tied, the values of Canadians and Americans are diverging rather than converging. Canada has continued along the road of tolerance and social justice for minorities in contrast to the America of recent years, which has increasingly come under the influence of the Religious Right.

It is hard to imagine now, but Canadians in the past were more religious than Americans. In the mid-1950s, 60 percent of Canadians said they attended church on Sunday compared with 50 percent of Americans. By the mid-1990s, church attendance had fallen to an average of 22 percent in Canada, whereas it still stood at 42 percent in the U.S. [1] Quebec, once the most conservative and churchgoing segment of society on the North American continent, has evolved into the most secular and postmodern region in Canada. It is modern Québécois culture, with its rejection of overarching religious power within the government, that is one of the key factors preventing Canada from succumbing to the political ambitions of the Religious Right. Canadians are now also far less deferential to a patriarchal form of authority, whether in the home or from the government. So the role of religion in a pluralistic country such as Canada is now essentially persuasive. Any form of threat or intimidation is counterproductive.

Core values of social liberalism increasingly distinguish Canada from the United States. Canada's national identity has been forged within a broad set of political and social objectives. With a history of holding together a disparate set of provincial values in confederation, and the pursuit of official bilingualism and a policy of multiculturalism — rather than the melting-pot ideal — Canadians have accumulated several decades of experience living in a pluralistic society with a strong culture of human rights. Canadians appear more at ease than Americans with the ambiguity and uncertainty that this produces.

Canadians do not want to live in a society that favours unfettered competition. Canadians have chosen to forego massive tax cuts in favour of preserving a social safety net, including a public health system for all, regardless of their ability to pay. "America," writes Adams, "honours traditionally masculine qualities; Canada honours qualities that are more traditionally feminine."[2] Canada has so far managed to preserve safeguards such as universal health care that provide social support for weaker members of the community. Compromise is the ideal, rather than rigid ideologies that lead to a win-lose social culture. Canadians generally embrace postmodern pluralism and reject flag-waving patriotism and overt religious intervention in the secular conduct of affairs.

The debate over same-sex marriage is pertinent here. South of the border, a debate over same-sex marriage has been hijacked in several states by referenda forbidding the passage of legislation on equal marriage. In Canada, Pierre Trudeau, the Jesuit-educated prime minister, had enshrined respect for minority rights in the Canadian constitution, which includes a Charter of Rights and Freedoms. The movement towards the recognition of equal marriage rights for gays and lesbians has flowed from that initiative.

On December 9, 2004, when the Supreme Court of Canada ruled that same-sex marriage was a constitutional right, the decision was defended by then prime minister Paul Martin and Ontario premier Dalton McGuinty. Both men are practising Catholics who are not afraid to resist pressure from the Church and call the bluff of Catholic bishops who had mounted a campaign against the legislation. In this instance, it seems to me that Martin and McGuinty represented what I have described as the Canadian movement towards a Magdalene Christianity, in sharp contrast to the macho churches of the American Religious Right, which carry more weight within the Republican party in the States. It also made Canada an increasingly desirable refuge for American gays and lesbians.

So while Canada's trading dependence on the United States remains a vital part of its economy, it does not appear that Canada's national distinctiveness has been eroded. Indeed, it may be becoming more pronounced. Canada now stands as a buffer zone to the erosion of social supports within the U.S. The time has come to stand firmly behind our belief in the importance of inclusivity, minority rights and the international order.

Canada could be the creative minority on the continent. A "model citizen," in the words of analyst Jennifer Welsh.[3] We are part of a circumpolar community at the northern edge of the earth's Arctic wilderness, but our southern border spans a series of dynamic and evolving urban communities, from Vancouver through Winnipeg, Toronto, and Montreal to Halifax. We have learned ways to maintain cohesion across one of the largest landmasses on earth without submerging the diversity of a pluralistic culture. In his book *The Rise of the Creative Class*, American economist Richard Florida outlines the three Ts that are key to the flourishing of cities in the twenty-first century: technology, tolerance and talent. Canada's three largest cities — Toronto, Montreal and Vancouver — all rank higher than any U.S. cities on this index.[4]

This assimilation of a diverse and potentially combustible population calls for the practice of what might be called a political and social asceticism, a frugality that accepts limits on the extent of national ostentation. Individualistic impulses are overcome in response to the twin demands of multiculturalism and the natural environment; thus Canadians are constantly reassessing their identity in the process of adjusting to the constraints of Canada's human and natural ecologies.

Making Canada work involves taking time and making the effort to adapt to the exigencies of forging an international consensus without the use of force. In the past fifty years, internationalism has also become a defining feature of Canadian identity. Almost one-fifth of the population in this generation — 18 percent — of Canadians are foreign-born.[5] A majority of Canadians favour more spending on overseas development and more engagement by the UN in international affairs. It was in 1971 that Canada became the first country in the world to create an official policy of multiculturalism. Toronto is fast becoming the most ethnically diverse city in the world.

Some sleeping dragons, though, still lurk beneath the surface of the vaunted Canadian mosaic. Despite an official affirmation of multiculturalism, there is still a tendency to define the Canadian identity as white and anglophone or francophone, and to refer to everyone else as "the others." Multicultural ethnicity is associated with non-whites and non-Christians, indicating that anglophones and francophones still hold the social centre. And multiculturalism in practice has often consisted of the addition of "ethnic" food (roast beef and mashed potatoes are never described as ethnic) and picturesque displays of "folk dance" as opposed to "classical" dance.

Moreover, calls for the tolerance of diversity can evoke a clash of values, and multiculturalism, as it turns out, may not include the advancement of feminism or gay rights. Canada's support of multiculturalism has been invoked by groups opposed to the universal principles of equality enshrined in the 1982 Charter of Rights and Freedoms. There are those who, on religious or cultural grounds, are reluctant to accept the concept of universal human rights as laid down in the charter. They have tried to resist the application of gender equality and homosexual rights within their communities by appealing to a grey area outlined in Section 27 of the Charter of Rights and Freedoms, which states that the courts are to interpret the Charter "in a manner consistent with the preservation and enhancement of the multicultural heritage of Canada," and the fundamental human rights enshrined in the Charter itself.[6]

Using the concept of human rights interpreted "in a manner consistent with the preservation of the multicultural heritage of Canada," groups opposed to the full inclusion of women and minorities have cited the protection of ethnic diversity (under the umbrella of multiculturalism) as the rationale for continuing certain forms of discrimination. The policy of multiculturalism has been misused as justification for exemption from the universal equal rights guaranteed under the Canadian Charter of Rights. Muslim parents in a Toronto public school attempted, unsuccessfully, to remove their children from classes promoting tolerance of gay and lesbian families. They argued that intolerance of homosexuality is a part of their culture as protected under Section 27 of the Charter and that the ethos of multiculturalism sanctioned their right to bring up their children in a manner consistent with their cultural prejudices.

Former prime minister Pierre Trudeau, the author of both the policy on multiculturalism and the Charter of Rights, would turn in his grave if he knew that its implementation would include the preservation of reactionary religious prejudices under the guise of fostering ethnic diversity. Gender equality and gay rights continue to be attacked by various ethnic and religious bodies claiming that such rights go against basic religious and cultural tenets in their communities and that their prejudice against certain groups or individuals is therefore protected by the Canadian Charter. But they have discovered that multiculturalism cannot override basic human rights guaranteed under the constitution. If human rights are truly universal, then they admit of no exceptions.

It is increasingly evident that those who argue on religious grounds against extending full human rights to certain groups, for example gays and lesbians, are caught on the horns of a dilemma. If human rights are God-given and universal, how is it that so many religious institutions still claim, in the name of the same God, to exclude certain groups from full equality, full humanity even? And when these religious traditions and secular rights collide, where does God stand? How can the divine claims of religion and divinely ordained universal human rights be in opposition? Exposing and resolving this question is one of the central tasks of this Magdalene moment.

Many religious traditionalists appear to be caught in a time warp. When religious teachings were first formulated, discrimination against women and homosexuals as well as ethnic minorities was universally accepted as a societal norm. But as democratic societies evolved and religious dictates no longer formed the basis of secular society, laws and value systems changed to the degree that misogyny and homophobia are now viewed as reprehensible.

How ironic it is that only after the separation of church and state have secular democratic governments, in the teeth of opposition from religiously affiliated groups, been able to promote the God-given equal rights of women and other historically marginalized groups. It is not surprising, then, that women today generally prefer to live under the protection offered by secular laws rather than be governed by religious or cultural laws. When the Canadian government, for example, began to restore the rights of self-governance to aboriginal groups — a laudable attempt to redress the effects of colonialism — aboriginal women spoke up in favour of living under the Canadian Constitution, which protects their right to equal treatment under the law, often in contrast to tribal laws, which tend to discriminate in favour of men.

In a secular democratic society, religious institutions are afforded the same freedom of speech as all other groups to disseminate their views. Paradoxically, the same Catholic Church that has ferociously resisted all attempts to introduce internal reforms towards democracy, freedom of expression or accountability within its own structures, now uses the right to free speech permitted within the public forum of secular Canadian democracy to advance religious arguments promoting intolerance and the denial of equal rights to women and homosexuals. In the early twentieth century the Catholic Church in Canada opposed the extension of suffrage to women. In the twenty-first, in addition to blocking the ordination of women to the priesthood in the church, the same Church has opposed the extension of equal civil rights in the secular sphere to gays and lesbians. To use arguments from multiculturalism and freedom of speech and religion to undermine human rights makes a mockery of the very democratic values that have allowed churches to exercise religious freedom in the first place.

The use of separate religious courts is another area where Charter rights have collided with interpretations of multiculturalism that favour the separate rights of ethnic minorities. In the fall of 2003 the Islamic Institute of Civil Justice in Ontario announced that it would start conducting arbitrations according to Islamic law. The president, Syed Mumtaz Ali, stated that "good Muslims" would be required to use this court. The 1991 arbitration law of Ontario allows Jewish Halacha and Muslim Sharia courts to function in place of secular courts within those communities. There was a great deal of negative public reaction to this announcement. Many Muslim groups as well as women's organizations expressed fear that women would be coerced into abrogating their equal rights under Canadian law by being forced to follow religious laws that discriminated against them. Women who had recently immigrated to Canada from countries where Sharia law is practised would be especially vulnerable because they might be unaware of their rights in Canada.

Former Ontario attorney general Marion Boyd was appointed to set up an inquiry and report to the government on the issues raised by the proposed introduction of Islamic religious law into the arbitration mechanism of the Province of Ontario. In December 2004 she released her findings, in which she stated that Muslim principles could be considered an acceptable method of religious arbitration in family disputes as long as they did not violate Canadian law.[7]

On September 11, 2005, in response to an overwhelmingly negative public response to this endorsement of religious arbitration courts, including the threat of revolt from the female members of the Liberal party caucus, Premier Dalton McGuinty announced that Ontario would end the use of all faith-based arbitration in separate religious courts. There would be one law for all women and men in Ontario, with no exceptions based on traditional beliefs or customs.

On May 26, 2005, the Quebec legislature had also passed a motion against the use of Sharia law within the legal system of the province. Arguing against the adoption of the law, a Muslim member of the Quebec legislature stated that the introduction of such courts represented the thin end of the wedge for fundamentalist groups who would seek to attack the foundations of democracy and equal rights for women in Canada. Furthermore, if a religious group tries to use the guarantee of freedom of religion under the Charter of Rights to claim exception to equality provisions, and thus discriminate internally against certain groups, this would amount to a perversion of the intent of the Charter. On a visit to Canada in June 2005, Shirin Ebadi of Iran denounced the attempts to introduce Sharia tribunals in Ontario and Quebec. Ebadi, who is the first Muslim woman to win the Nobel Peace Prize, stated that religious tribunals undermine democratic values and human rights.[8]

The irony, even the tragedy, of the present moment is that secular governments have been the first to recognize the God-given human rights of women and minorities. Religious leaders, who preach the oneness of the human made in the image of the Creator, resist putting this teaching into practice within their own structures. Now, they are using the open and inclusive structures of democratic societies such as Canada to invade the secular realm and try to restrict the rights of others.

But do they really speak for God? Where is God, and how does God speak today? And what is the place of religion in a pluralistic society?

Back to that dusky Harbourfront evening, where every so often Youssou N'Dour inserts a song with a decidedly Arab flavour into the program, reflecting his recent interest in Sufi mysticism. I close my eyes for a minute and hear echoes of the haunting call of the muezzin from a nearby mosque in the early hours of the morning when I have woken up in various places in Africa — in Lagos, Nigeria; in Kumbo N'So, Cameroon; and more recently in Durban, South Africa.

A word I often heard in South Africa was *ubuntu*. Literally, *ubuntu* means being bound up together. It means that we cannot exist apart from our relationships with others. I am, only because you are. Regardless of race or religion, we are all bound up together as a human race in a close-knit cluster of interdependence with all earth's creatures. That interdependence, that absolute necessity of relationship, is the spark of divinity that exists within all created life.

Before Youssou N'Dour came on stage, Achilla Orru, a Ugandan musician now based in Toronto, played a set. Blind from birth, Achilla Orru is an extraordinarily gifted singer. He plays the lokembe, a thumb piano that is a traditional instrument of the Karimojong people. A few years ago I had the privilege of living with Grace, a Karimojong refugee from the Gulu district in Uganda, who is now part of Orru's backup group. I recalled an occasion when Achilla Orru came to my house to celebrate Grace's birthday.

Over the past fifteen years, my house has been a reflection of the city of Toronto, where people from every continent (except Australia, so far!) have lived together under the same roof. It is they who have taught me about *ubuntu*. Several people share the communal kitchen, so we customarily label any food in the refrigerator with the initials of its owner. Grace refused to label the food she placed in the fridge. For her, sharing food was an intrinsic way of living in community because, as she put it, food exists for the purpose of appeasing the hunger of whoever needs it. This was a severe challenge for the rest of us because it upset the personal boundaries and property rights that Canadians take for granted. We eventually reached a compromise whereby we all decided to share more of our food, and so we designated a certain area in the fridge for that purpose.

To foster a cross-cultural community in which people from many different backgrounds share the same roof demands a constant "de-centring" of the self. A certain elasticity develops where the need for safe space, the drawing of boundaries of security, and the demands of relationality intersect. As we adapt to change and to challenging situations, a flow of reciprocity grows in the community. For Christians, this kind of give and take reflects the pattern at the heart of the great mystery called the Holy Trinity: one God in three persons engaged in unconditional love and self-giving. A God whose very being is *ubuntu*. A God to whom relationship is the stuff of existence, and who does not exist, to use an old theological term, *in se* (in God's own nature and God's self) or *ad extra* (in relationship with creation), except in *ubuntu*.

At this moment in history, we have the knowledge and technological means to take a giant step toward a more radical reciprocity and to practise *ubuntu* with creation and with all of humanity. This is a Magdalene moment, a God-sent opportunity. If we are to work together as a human community to save the earth and its creatures, the religions of the world must undergo deep transformation before they can join in God's great work for our age. The new cosmology outlined in Chapter 3 has dramatically changed the way we view the relationship of heaven and earth. Creation is no longer an inanimate pile of rocks at the bottom of a pyramid of ascending importance, with male humanity set at its apex to rule all other categories of being. The human species is part of an intricate circle of life that is nonhierarchical and interdependent.

The human race is at a crucial moment in its history. Across the globe, refugees are being driven from their homes by local and international strife of various kinds. The wars that plague so many areas of the world are not directly religious in origin but they have often been made more intractable by the use of religious teachings, language and symbolism. Environmental destruction, the plight of women and girls, poverty and disease are interdependent and often directly related to traditional religious teachings. The sacred scriptures that form the basis of the laws and practices of all Western contemporary religious groups were written with a premodern consciousness. Even though the sacred writings of all religions contain strands of universalism and inclusiveness, more often than not they envisage God as the exclusive possession of certain groups who are in competition with other groups for adherents and power. It is time for religions to stop competing among themselves and to acknowledge that maybe God actually delights in the diversity of religious traditions that have arisen within human history in response to God's revelation.

The new cosmology, which points to the unity of all life within and outside the planet, could be the inspiration for a new direction for the religions of the world. It is unlikely that such a vision will arise from the staid and orchestrated gatherings of religious leaders, who have too much at stake in maintaining the status quo to risk taking an imaginative leap forward into a new paradigm. No — this spiritual renewal will be a Magdalene movement from the margins, led for the most part by women.

"As a woman I have no country. As a woman I want no country. As a woman my country is the whole world." This quotation from Virginia Woolf's story "Three Guineas" appears at the beginning of Jane Schaberg's *The Resurrection of Mary Magdalene*. Schaberg continues: "She [Woolf] can teach us to say, As a woman I have no religion. I am not a Jew or a Christian or a pagan — a view which may bring us closer to appreciating first century CE pluralisms and identity constructions as well as possibilities for the future."[9]

The question of religious pluralism touches the very heart and soul of belief. Is there one human race, which has evolved under the creative artistry of one and the same God and is beloved by this God? Is God for all human beings, or only for one particular group? Does God choose only some kinds of people and reject others? And if there are true religions and false religions, then who defines which is true and which false? And a crucial question for Christians is: does God effect salvation only through Jesus Christ?

When the late Pope John Paul II lay dying in February 2005, a little Muslim girl who was also ill wrote him a letter. In the letter, she mentioned that she would pray to Allah for him. I remember wondering at the time: how will Allah look upon this prayer for the Pope, the head of a competing and sometimes militantly hostile religion? Is her Allah the same as the Pope's God? Do both Allah and Jesus want the Pope to go to heaven? These questions verge on the ridiculous when stated so baldly. And indeed they are absurd when placed in the context of the very real suffering of two human beings. When placed in the context of suffering humanity, religious rivalries appear petty and inconsequential. The cries of humanity and of creation in crisis overwhelm paltry concerns about doctrine and exclusive salvation.

The Koran contains a beautiful teaching about the origin of humanity. It says that God created different races so that they could vie with each other in compassion. "If God had so willed, He would have made all of you one community, but He has not done that so that He may test you in what He has given you; so compete in goodness. To God shall you all return, and He will tell you the truth about what you have been disputing."[10] Had Islamic and other religious leaders followed that irenic vision of the Koran, which is very close to the vision of the prophets in the Hebrew Scriptures and the teachings of Jesus, then religions might have assumed a very different posture from the militant aggression of one toward another that has plagued the world for centuries. Who now dares to parcel out God into different religious packages and seal them with a fallible human understanding, knowing from historical experience that such a seal will be broken open in the next generation?

Thomas Aquinas, the medieval theologian whose writings have formed the basis of much of classical Christian theology, had the following insight:

For God brought all things into being in order that His goodness might be communicated to creatures and be represented
by them, because his goodness could not be represented
adequately by one creature alone ... for the goodness which
in God is simple and uniform, in creatures is manifold and
divided; hence the whole universe together participates in
the divine goodness more perfectly and represents it better
than any single creature whatsoever.[11]

Intra-religious strife has left deep scars in human history.
Exclusivist religious ideologies have led to the genocide of
indigenous peoples, ethnic cleansing, and decades of civil war
in Northern Ireland and the Middle East. It goes without saying that exclusivist ideologies exacerbate the current wave of
global terrorism. The emergence of the militant right wing in
Islam has been paralleled by the growth of the reactionary
Christian Right in U.S. Protestantism and the retrogressive
turn of the Catholic papacy. There are many complex reasons
for this, some of which are connected to economic and political realities. But this sharp shift to the right is also in part a
reaction to the overarching influence of postmodernity.

Postmodernism has ushered in a revolution in cultural
and social awareness. History is no longer viewed from
the vantage point of the winners, or as an inevitable march
toward progress. The European "discovery" of the Americas,
for example, is now no longer viewed as part of a divine
plan for bringing enlightenment and salvation to its pagan
indigenous inhabitants. Europeans who lived at the time,

with the exception of prescient individuals such as Bartolome de las Casas,[12] viewed themselves as a superior race of humans with a divine destiny to conquer the world and spread the gospel. Now these and similar assumptions have come under severe critique. The genocide of indigenous peoples at the hands of Christian missionaries, and the suppression of aboriginal spirituality, are now seen as crimes against the Creator in whose image they are equally made and whose wisdom they had so deeply imbibed.

The postmodern shift in cultural and cosmic awareness has come about through the emergence of hitherto marginalized groups, such as women and previously colonized peoples, into mainstream academic and political discourse. This has affected theology as much as other disciplines, although churches have lagged behind other social groups in accommodating the new consciousness of groups previously deemed to be of less significance in their divinely ordained hierarchy of being. To a large extent the God of Christianity is still envisaged as white, male, and supportive of Western culture and capitalist economics.

In reaction to the ambivalence of the postmodern moment and the questioning and breakdown of traditional structures, believers have reacted in different ways. On the one hand are those who view the postmodern ethos as at best a threat and at worst a harbinger of a total breakdown in the fabric of society. They deal with this by retreating into strident dogmatism and rigid observance of traditional religious practices. The certainties of Christian exclusivism have become more attractive as a bulwark against perceived anarchy. Those threatened by postmodernity seek to create purer, more definitive versions of their various affiliations, casting nostalgic glances back to the halcyon days when God was in his heaven, and when obeying church rules and going to church services on Sunday would fulfill religious obligations and guarantee life everlasting.

On the other side are those who argue that the present crisis is a prelude to a new and inevitable breakthrough in human consciousness. Our understanding of God is evolving under the influence of the new cosmology, as science becomes a new path to mysticism. We lack the words or means of worship to reflect this new knowledge and experience adequately, but we nonetheless sense that old rituals and myths, though deeply cherished, are inadequate, and that our previous understanding of God was limiting.

James Fowler, a psychologist who has done considerable work in the psycho-social analysis of faith development, argues that religious reactions to the impact of postmodernism reflect different stages of faith development.[13] These cycles of development are not necessarily in lock-step, one following another. Sometimes they can be cyclical — we can go in and out of them as we react to varying life experiences.

In adolescence, religious belief is often articulated in doctrinaire or absolutist terms. Everything is viewed in black and white. A person is either part of the in-group or outside it — and who does not remember that teenage dread of being shunned by a peer group? A kind of tribal consciousness takes over, and membership in the group exacts a high degree of conformity to an externally validated code. Loyalty to the group often results in viciously personal attacks on those whose ideas or actions appear to threaten communal cohesion. Other characteristics are a strong sense of personal idealism and hero-worship of those who model the accepted values of the group.

Soon after he became Pope on April 19, 2005, Benedict XVI announced his preference for a pared-down, purer Catholic Church, where his version of doctrine will be meticulously and unquestioningly observed. This appeals to Catholics who prefer to remain in, or revert to, an adolescent stage of belief rather than stepping into the uncertainties of spiritual adulthood. The notion of the Rapture in American evangelical Christianity, in which only a few chosen souls are saved and the rest perish into eternal damnation, is a similar example of an adolescent level of faith.

In the transition to adulthood, some kind of crisis inevitably upsets this ordered universe. The external supports for a person's faith will often fail in one way or another. It could be that a significant role model or a member of the in-group betrays the ideals upon which the faith appears to be based, or that a breakdown in a personal or family relationship causes a questioning of the existence of God as hitherto defined. For some, this may result in the temporary or permanent abandonment of belief in God.

But out of this crisis there may emerge an adult level of faith. An adult is able to live with ambiguity, to reflect on truth in the light of personal experience and appreciate a vulnerability in the self and in others in a way that helps to overcome the self-righteous rigidity of the adolescent. The ability develops to reach out to those outside a narrowly defined group of doctrinaire purists and interact with a more diverse circle.

Although some believers are retreating into fundamentalism, the human race as a whole is currently struggling to pass from the adolescence of competitive, dogmatic institutionalized religions into an adult phase of spiritual development. This is a difficult and painful journey. Who among us has not experienced at one time or another a deep loneliness and sense of alienation in the postmodern world, which has resulted from the breakdown of so many spheres of life and the dysfunction of religious institutions? But unless we put aside the yearning for absolute certainty, the need for a magician God — a *deus ex machina* in the sky — and the missionary zeal to convert the other to our particular way of thinking, mutual tolerance and compassion will diminish.

Religious teachings developed during a period when human knowledge about the cosmos was limited. The old cosmology has been discredited, but the ancient concepts of God endure. In readings and prayers still used in religious rituals today, God is addressed as male, all-powerful and often vengeful and punitive, seated literally on a celestial throne in some realm completely cut off from the earth. These traditional images of God have become too narrow for the new vision of the divine. Yet to tamper with traditional ritual and language is fraught with ambivalence and controversy.

In secular societies, policies have been enacted to address the inequities perpetuated in, for example, language, by moving to the usage of inclusive pronouns. Religious institutions not only lag behind in addressing structural gender inequities but in many cases resist even small steps toward addressing the problem, by insisting on the use of exclusively male terms in the liturgy. Add to this a general sense of social dislocation and the awareness of massive global poverty, and it is little wonder that many people today experience a deep sadness, a residual ambiguity of soul and a longing for spiritual comfort.

The new cosmic spirituality encompasses diverse threads in creative tension. Multiple perspectives are taken into account within a cosmology in which the fundamental trajectory of the universe is toward connection and relationship rather than competition, hierarchy and exclusion. This Magdalene movement is happening within Christianity, mostly at the margins. It is also happening in other faith groups, particularly among women, who have less of a stake in traditional religious power structures. This breaking out of the narrow bonds of traditional dogma will allow God to be God again.

Religions throughout the ages have celebrated the connection of humanity and the divine. Humanity knew and worshipped a God with multiple dimensions long before the Christian theology of God as a Trinity of being was defined. It was from observations of the cosmos itself that humanity first elicited intimations of the divine. The fluctuations of the seasons, the energy of wind, water and air, the fertility of the earth, and the cycles of sex, birth and death in animal and human life were all intimations of the immanent but transcendent power of God. The power and relationship inherent within creation revealed the mystery of God that was later formalized into religious ritual and observance. Creation was awake with the glory of God long before humans developed the power of art and language to articulate this.

Over the centuries, religious dogma served to alienate humanity from the earth and engender competition as rival groups fought over competing definitions of the divine. The time has come to put aside these divisions and to discover once again the one God who is greater than any human definition. Christian teaching on the Trinity is an attempt to articulate the human experience of God. The whole notion of God as a Trinity of being implies that God exists in diversity, in limitless relationship. And thus the Trinity offers great possibilities, not least in the crucial issue of religious pluralism. God as a Trinity of Being reflects the core belief that relationship is the key to God's essence. Every relationship is a two-fold process: the giving of the self and the receiving of the other. This self-giving love supports and does not destroy the identity of the other. But in a relationship of mutual love, the identity of each person takes on a new dimension; while remaining distinct, it cannot be fully defined apart from the other. It is only in giving themselves away that the individuals absorbed in a relationship become more centred in their own identities.

Anyone who has experienced true love knows the risks involved in the giving to, and receiving from, another. Love allows each partner to be who she or he is. But both partners are open to being changed by the relationship: to make a common ground where a third reality, born of reciprocal love, can be created out of their mutual self-giving. Then we begin to harbour within ourselves the ones to whom we give ourselves away in love. Mutual sexual relationships approximate most closely the dynamic and open love that exists within God. Partners in a sexual relationship do not dissolve into each other, but the fusion of their bodies and souls changes the way they operate within the wider world, both individually and as a couple. They act and are acted upon at one and the same time. This is both the vulnerability and beauty of healthy sexual loving, which is patterned on God's very being.

I cannot ever say that I possess a friend or a lover in a controlling way. An individual's identity is not submerged in the relationship, and while both lover and beloved are in a dynamic movement toward each other, they are also held within the context of the world beyond the boundary of their embrace. Thus their love is directed internally, within the relationship, and also externally, toward the world beyond.

It is mystics and lovers who understand best the mystery at the heart of the unity and diversity that is God. "The almighty truth of the Trinity is our Father, for he made us and keeps us in him. And the deep wisdom of the Trinity is our Mother, in whom we are enclosed. And the high goodness of the Trinity is our Lord, and in him we are enclosed and he in us."[14] The Trinity is a never-ending process of mutual and unconditional love within God. In the traditional language, the Trinity has been described as Father, Son and Holy Ghost.

This may have served its purpose in previous centuries, but this terminology is inadequate for our age. Many believers today substitute terms such as Creator for Father; Redeemer, Word or Wisdom for Son; and *Ruach* or Breath of God for Spirit.

The theological term for divine love is "perichoresis," a Greek word meaning the "mutual indwelling" that results from self-giving love. God is not static and self-enclosed but, rather, open and dynamic. The pattern of self-giving love within the Trinity furnishes a model of abandoning egocentrism and exclusivity. It means the opening up of the self to the other, allowing the other to find space within the self and being open to change. This has important consequences on a number of levels, including contemporary explorations of gender identity and religious pluralism. The three persons within one nature is a prototype for relationships between the sexes. "The one triune God in whose image all human beings are created holds the promise of peace between men and women with irreducible but changing gender identities."[15] Gender identity and patterns of relationships cannot be frozen into particular cultural understandings.

This Trinitarian understanding of God provides a model of radical openness on a universal level as well. As the human face of God, Jesus proclaimed the divine love for the "other" — the stranger, the poor, the one who is not like us. The call of Jesus was to leave the familiarity of home and the fisherman's shore and form a new community that was not based on externally determined identities. That call echoes across the centuries to the present. The identity of Jesus in the

Scriptures was initially manifested as the fulfillment of a genealogical promise to Abraham and Sara, but Jesus' life and teaching marked the end of genealogy as a guarantee of privileged access to God. Jesus refused to privilege any ethnicity, class or gender as chosen by God. In a remarkable scene included in the gospels of both Mark and Matthew, Jesus' understanding of his own identity was reshaped by the intervention of a woman. A Canaanite woman comes to beg Jesus to heal her daughter. He rudely dismisses her entreaty, saying that his gifts are not to be thrown to foreign dogs like herself. But after her repeated cries for help, he recognizes within her the voice of God speaking through an unexpected source, a woman and a foreigner. After curing her daughter and praising her faith, he goes into Gentile territory on the other side of the Sea of Galilee and feeds four thousand people.[16]

These two incidents are a powerful sign that even the consciousness of Jesus was open to change and evolution in self-understanding. He was sent to save not only the House of Israel, but the world in all its vastness and diversity. I believe that an evolution in the relationship of Christians with God is taking place today. Not only have Christian churches been challenged to welcome the poor, women, and homosexuals, but now the voice of the Canaanite woman, the consummate outsider by reason of race, gender and religion, is being heard in the call to recognize the presence and activity of God within other religions as well as our own.

Contemporary theological developments in the articulation of the Trinitarian understanding of God have opened the door to a renewed understanding and appreciation of religious pluralism. One of the major areas of contention here is the question of how Christians, without abandoning their belief in Jesus Christ, can honour the ways in which God has revealed divinity through paths followed by other religions. This in turn is linked to another question of critical importance: how do we struggle to change exclusive definitions of religious identity without surrendering to an amorphous anarchy or chaos that could provide fertile ground for a return to fundamentalism or fascism?

In Christian terms, our identity is constantly shifting as we are decentred by baptism and recentred on the risen Christ. The new identity does not obliterate the self but recentres it in love, thus opening a new threshold in the heart that is challenged to look at the other, be that an individual or a group, through the eyes of God, beyond all cultural and religious prejudices. God's will is to save and to love, not to condemn. How could such a God foster discrimination and prejudice? The pattern of God's self-giving love reaches a crucial point with the life, death and resurrection of Jesus of Nazareth. The humanity of God manifested in Jesus does not clothe itself in the sword of missionary zeal or the shield of religious dogma but in a naked body and outstretched arms on the cross. The vulnerability of Jesus is part of the risk of God's unconditional love. Diverse religions have evolved in different regions, most of them pre-dating Christianity by centuries, if not millennia. The question now arises as to the relationship between all these religions. Do all religions represent equally valid understandings of God? Can Christians still claim that Jesus Christ is the one and universal Saviour of humankind, whether overtly Christian or not? Does that mean that God has geographical or ethnic preferences? But if so, how can God punish people who, through no fault of their own, did not acknowledge Christ? And who cannot but be scandalized by the centuries of violence inflicted by Christians on those they called pagans or infidels? Their dangerous notion of an exclusivist God cannot be supported today.

The Creator, the Word and Spirit of God — three in one — set in motion the outpouring of energy that bodied forth the universe approximately 15 billion years ago. The creation myths incorporated into the early Hebrew Scriptures emphasize a God who sought relationship with humanity. In that beautiful phrase of the third chapter of Genesis, God came seeking Adam and Eve in the Garden in the cool of the evening: "That evening, they heard the Lord God walking in the garden."[17] Religious pluralism is a reflection of the variety of ways in which, since the beginning of time, God has sought relationship with all of humanity as represented by this loving metaphorical embrace of our common parents.

It is through an evolving understanding of the Trinity that Christians can achieve a new awareness of the breadth and depth of God's activity in the world, which is not confined to God's revelation through Jesus Christ. God certainly offers a way to share in divine eternal life and infinite love through Jesus. Christ was the full presence of God within history. Jesus translated into words and deeds the mystery of God.

But God was active in the world before the birth of Jesus. The particular historical events of the life, death and resurrection of Jesus Christ do not represent the sum total of God's revelation to humanity.

The essence of the Trinitarian God is greater than the revelation of God within the person of Jesus Christ. If Christians begin to locate the particularity of Jesus within the universality of God's self-revelation, rather than placing God's universality within the particularity of the historical Jesus, they can open the path to a true religious pluralism. Jesus called people to the fullness of life rather than to a specific religion. Let us acknowledge that Christians are co-pilgrims in human history alongside others. The Spirit of God, the *ruach* who moved over and stirred the waters of creation, has been universally present in human history both before and after the earthly life of Jesus.

The Spirit, the third person of the Trinity, is also the full presence of God in history. The Spirit appears in forms that are non-gendered and hard to pin down in dogmatic terms: fire, wind, breath, a dove. It is impossible to domesticate this Spirit or channel the Spirit within the boundaries of institutions. To quote the Ecumenical Consultation at Baar, Switzerland:

> We see the plurality of religious traditions as both a result of the manifold ways in which God has related to peoples and nations as well as a manifestation of the riches and diversity of humankind. We affirm that God has been present in their seeking and finding, that where there is truth and wisdom in

their teachings and love and holiness in their living ... this is the gift of the Holy Spirit. We also affirm that God is with them as they struggle, along with us, for justice and liberation.

This conviction that God as Creator of all is present and active in the plurality of religions makes it inconceivable to us that God's saving activity could be confined to any continent, culture type or groups of people.[18]

God's countenance assumes an infinite number of features. Jesus the Jew often travelled at the margins of the religious orthodoxy of his time. To be truly open to the religious tradition of another means crossing over into uncharted territory. To find a place of spiritual peace between warring religious parties, a peace the world so desperately needs, we need to open the boundaries of self-enclosed traditions. By meeting in a common space, with no fixed boundaries, two separate traditions can be enriched. The new mutual awareness that emerges will be different from anything that was there before the meeting. To see the complexity of truth requires a double vision: to see it "from there" as well as "from here."

Allegiance to God in our day demands that we have the courage to step into this uncharted territory to meet God. The mothering spirit of God that brooded over creation moved the waters, and they surged into life. The great stream of the waters of life flowed into multiple oceans and rivers. The goddess Sul's pool, which I visited in Bath, the River Jordan, the Ganges — all sacred waters flow from the same stream of the Spirit into a diversity of outlets. Other religions that came under the mothering wings of the same Spirit of God have drunk deeply of these waters of life. God alights in the misty territory of unregulated spirituality, an encounter as elusive as a breeze and yet as firm as the granite of the Canadian Shield.

> The religions of the world are expressions of human openness to God. They are signs of God's presence in the world. Each religion is unique, and through this uniqueness, religions enrich each other. In their specificity, they manifest different faces of the supreme Mystery which is never exhausted. In their diversity, they enable us to experience the richness of the One more profoundly.[19]

This statement is from the Indian Theological Association. It states clearly that pluralism does not mean that religions should dissolve into a mushy soup of relativism, where the salt of each loses its savour. Pluralism assumes a commitment to one's own tradition, but with an understanding that even matters that are held as divinely ordained and universally applicable are limited because they are the product of a particular conception and world view. Within this common ground — of partnership rather than competition — the divine can be experienced in all its richness.

The Christian theology of religious pluralism is gradually evolving from exclusivism (the belief that only Christians can be saved) to an ever-widening inclusivism. There was a time in the Middle Ages and beyond when the Catholic Church taught that *extra ecclesiam nulla salus*: that is, without belonging to the Catholic Church a person could not be saved and would therefore be condemned to hell. The Christ of this imperial church was set up over and against all other religions. The Crusades, the Inquisition and other forced conversions of aboriginal peoples manifested the ugly face of this teaching, which held sway for more than a thousand years.

What drove the final nail into the coffin of the *extra ecclesiam nulla salus* teaching was the need to atone for the shameful silence of so many Christians in Europe in the face of the Nazi Holocaust. How could the Christian community continue to claim that it offered the only valid way to God after it had failed so lamentably to condemn so great an evil and, to a considerable extent, had actively cooperated in its perpetration? Following this recognition, the 1950s and 60s saw a shift in the theological understanding of the relationship of Christianity to other faiths. The notion of the "anonymous Christian" was introduced in the writings of the German theologian Karl Rahner, who was an adviser to the Second Vatican Council.

The influence of Rahner, whose *Theological Investigations* — a twenty-three-volume collection of his talks, lectures and writings — had a major impact on Catholic theology during and after the Second Vatican Council, has been compared to that of Karl Barth or Paul Tillich in the Protestant world. Rahner set out to explore ways of recovering the meaning of Christian theology in an intellectual framework that was plausible in the contemporary world. Although the mystery of God, in his view, always exceeded human reach, God could be known through creation and human experience. Rahner believed that although Christ was the supreme revelation of God in human history, God's Spirit had been at work in the world since the first moment of creation, encouraging the human spirit toward truth and goodness. Any person who responds to the needs of the world with love and generosity makes what Rahner referred to as a fundamental option for God, even though he or she may not affirm God's existence.

Following Rahner's lead, other theologians began accepting that God loves and saves people of goodwill in other religions. Though they still clung to the notion of an exclusively Christian God, they argued that people could be saved by Christ even though they did not know Christ or follow Christian teachings: if they were good people, they were anonymous Christians in spite of themselves. In other words, even though the majority of humankind is not baptized into the Christian community, Jesus is still the unique and normative channel for their relationship with God. They still have to go to God through Jesus even though they themselves are unaware of this exigency. This view still clings to the notion of an exclusively Christian God. Though not as ruthless as the previous teaching that no one can be saved who is not a member of the Catholic Church, it is still a paternalistic attitude and would doubtless be vigorously rejected by those to whom it applied.

The idea of the anonymous Christian represents a step in the right direction—away from the idea that God would assign all non-Christians, witting or unwitting, to hell. But it still rested on the assumption that God wills the entire human population to be saved only on Christian terms, not by virtue of their own religious beliefs, and that other religious beliefs will ultimately be subsumed into Christianity. It still places Christianity at the centre of God's revelation, with all others on the periphery.

In more recent times, even this modified Christian exclusivism has become an inadequate vehicle to convey the new understanding of God that is now emerging. While postmodern analysis has exposed the tenuous nature of truth and the limitations of previous claims to infallibility, science — particularly the theory of evolution and the new cosmology — has opened the way to the belief that God is greater than any time-bound human conceptualization, and that humanity's understanding of God, like humanity itself, is a work in process. The revolution in communications and increasing access to the internet have enabled a global cross-cultural dialogue and exchange of views. The worldwide movement of refugees and immigrants has meant that people who were previously strangers to one another's religions may now share neighbourhoods, and their children may go to the same schools. Though this process is not without tension and conflict, religious pluralism is a fact of life for an increasing number of people. And when new human experience confronts outdated religious tenets, then ultimately experience leads to a change in belief.

The realities of women's lives often place them on the cusp of these changes. Women themselves have suffered marginalization for centuries by being subsumed into male humanity. Definitions of the nature of God have reflected the projections of patriarchal societies, where women have been excluded from religious office and thus from close approximation to the divine. Until very recently, men were the norm, and women had to fit into their world. Because of their experience of non-identity in relation to God, women now are in a unique position to lead the necessary deconstruction of religious ideologies and structures that inhibit the embrace of true religious pluralism. Traditional language about God has hitherto offered women few avenues of identification with divinity. At this Magdalene moment, women are now recovering their lost sense of divinity.

Women have far less at stake in the preservation of competing and patriarchal religious traditions. As outsiders themselves, they inhabit the margins of patriarchal religious structures. It is here that the Spirit of God is working to renew the earth. We are just beginning to feel the impact of the evolution of the role of women in religious structures, and the relationship of women to the divine. Women for the most part are still outsiders to the formal interfaith dialogues that have taken place in recent years, but it is not through these formal high-level diplomatic negotiations that the change will come. The acceptance — nay, even the rejoicing in religious plural- ism and diversity — is a movement that is already under way at the margins of the institutions. Until recently, the voices of women have not been heard within the structures of the world's religions, even though it is women by and large who have sustained those structures by their presence and work. In the Magdalene movement, women are leading the way toward finding common ground based on a shared concern for cosmic survival rather than competitive power structures.[20]

Any species-wide effort to "power down" in order to save the earth must include religion. A species-wide effort toward self-limitation through reduction in consumption and a limitation of population growth is required no less in the religious than in the economic and social sphere. This Magdalene moment calls for a new asceticism within religion itself: a humble, almost frugal dynamic as opposed to aggressive proselytizing, competition for power and insistence on exclusive proprietary rights over God.

The contemporary crisis of earth and humanity provides the motivation for religions to find common ground in the face of eco/human suffering. More than a hundred years ago, in 1893, Charles Bonney, one of the leading lights in the fledgling interfaith movement, wrote: "Henceforth the religions of the world will make war not on each other but on the giant evils that afflict mankind."[21] This dream will only be realized when human imagination makes room for the new understanding of God that is emerging in our time.

I have come into the world to hear this:

every song the earth has sung since it was conceived in
the Divine's womb and began spinning from
His wish,

every song by wing and fin and hoof,
every song by hill and field and tree and woman and child,
every song of stream and rock,

every song of tool and lyre and flute,
every song of gold and emerald
and fire,

every song the heart should cry with magnificent dignity
to know itself as
God;

For all other knowledge will leave us again in want and aching-
only imbibing the glorious Sun
will complete us.

I have come into the world to see this:
the sword drop from men's hands
even at the height of
their arc of
rage

because we have finally realized
there is just one flesh

we can wound.

— FROM HAFIZ,
"I HAVE COME INTO THE WORLD TO SEE THIS"[22]

Epilogue

IN 1992, soon after the outbreak of the Balkan war of 1991–1995, stories began to surface of the mass rapes of Muslim women in Bosnia by Serbian Christian soldiers. Analysts distinguished three kinds of rape in Bosnia: rapes that occurred when Serbs first occupied a village; rapes committed by Serbian and Croatian prison guards in detention camps; and rape camps, or temporarily commandeered houses, where Serbs kept Muslim women expressly for that purpose. These reports also emphasized that rapes often took place in public or in front of other witnesses; that rapes included acts designed to degrade the victim; and that often the victims knew their aggressors.

Religion had defined the ethnic strife in this conflict: Islamic, Roman Catholic and Orthodox Christian — and religious antagonism contributed to the violence on all sides. But whose God heard the cries of the rape victims? In traditional Islam,

Roman Catholicism and Orthodox Christianity, there is no maternal face of God. Women cannot represent the divine, and they are subordinate to men in all things sacred. When religion affirms male humanity as superior to female, it affords some men additional reason to hold women in contempt and to inflict violence on them. In the Balkan war, religion was not the only element that shaped the conflict, but it exacerbated it.

Laurie Buchanan, who taught in the English department at Humber College, worked with me in the brief but intense five-year effort to reform the Canadian Catholic Church initiated by the Coalition of Concerned Canadian Catholics (CCCC). She had the inspiration that in multicultural Toronto, women could play a unique role in responding to this crisis. The terrible suffering inflicted on women as a result of war could motivate women to make common cause in an effort to put an end to historical rivalries and the violence these engender.

We formed a group with Muslim, Serbian Orthodox, Catholic, Protestant, Jewish, aboriginal and Hindu women. We called it the Women's Multifaith Coalition. None of us had any official title or position within any religious communities. Yet in the course of a year of meetings we managed to sustain this fragile and sometimes fractious working group. We discovered that we could pray together to one God, and in doing so, we crossed a threshold into the mystery of a God beyond gender, race or religion. By working together on this common project, we women from differing religious and ethnic identities began to understand and accept one another. Despite our differences, we developed authentic speech, not a message that had been imposed upon us by religious traditions hostile to women's spiritual emancipation. We realized, to paraphrase the statement of Virginia Woolf quoted in the previous chapter, that as women we wanted no country, no religion: for our country, we wanted the whole world, and for our religion, we wanted an inclusive God whose divinity embraces women.

It was new territory for us all. Sometimes it felt as though we were stepping on eggshells, at other times on minefields. Yet focused on the exigencies of our common struggle, we found that we were able to work together. We shared the experience of exclusion from religious power. This awareness that religion was often used against us as a means of subjugation helped us to identify with the victims on all sides of this war. We began to realize that the spiritual betrayal of one of us affected all of us, and that we had to become the guardians of each other's rights. We also began to see ourselves and our traditions through one another's eyes.

As women linked by concern for the suffering of the world, we entered a liminal space where a new world is taking shape and a new spirituality of global interdependence is being forged. In the Women's Multifaith Coalition, marginalized women found a strong sense of relationship that overcame the divisions among our warring traditions. With no rules to constrain us, we had crossed into a new space where we could allow ourselves to be seen through the eyes of the others, where we allowed the others to feed back to us the way they saw our traditions from their vantage points. In so doing, we absorbed some of their thinking about our own traditions and became changed in the process. From this new place of existence, we were able to construct a common ground of prayer in which we all addressed the one God who is greater than the sum of all our individual traditions put together. We were able to forge this unity because our prayer was not uttered in the abstract; it was called forth by the urgent need to respond to the cries of the suffering world.

Laurie Buchanan took an unpaid leave of absence from teaching to coordinate the project, which we named "Woman to Woman." We put out an appeal for supplies to be sent in care packages to women prisoners of war on all sides of the Balkan conflict. Within three months, we received more than a hundred-thousand dollars' worth of supplies from all over Canada, which were packaged into about two thousand cotton bags that had also been donated.

Our efforts culminated in a packed, emotionally charged public service held at Toronto's City Hall on February 14, 1993, led by women of various faiths, united in their concern to end the rape of women as an act of war. As one woman from Canada's First Nations lit the sacred fire, we prayed: "O flaming Spirit of love, we cry out to you in the midst of the struggles of our lives. O Holy One, hear our cry. We offer to you our broken sisterhood. Help us to remember the wholeness that you intended." For a brief moment, we were able to imagine that a different world was possible.

History is shaped by memories. But all history is partial. Our interpretation of the past is always fragmented — shaped by the interests we pursue and filtered through the cultures and traditions we inhabit. The past can shed light on the present, but the injustices done to the dead should not be allowed to perpetuate conflicts between the living.

Around the world, those on the margins who have been disempowered by sexism and other patriarchal restrictions are finding their voices. In the new cosmology, science has stretched our understanding of creation and the universe. A basic law of nature is that all species are enriched, not threatened, by diversity. Now, we are beginning to recognize that what unites us as human beings is greater than our historical divisions.

Our spiritual allegiance now lies with God's future: one that is open to the outpouring of the Spirit into the world, beyond the bondage of our hidebound institutions and beyond religious rivalries. This does not mean that religious identity will be lost, but rather that religious competition will be abandoned in favour of finding a new common ground of compassion. Drawing on the depths of mercy and love within each religious tradition, is it not possible to open up a common pool of compassion? All religions have been animated by the divine. Is it not possible to admit the limitations of the different versions of God that humans have projected onto the divine? This understanding of diversity would enrich rather than threaten the appreciation of the divine. Our concept of God has become too small, and the nets of traditional religious institutions too confining, for the revelation of God that is occurring in our age. Just as there are no generic human beings, so there are no generic revelations of God. There is no one big truth about God; there are only multiple perspectives. We cannot continue to sacrifice one another at the altars of our differing religious truths by retreating into theological fundamentalism. Jesus, the witness to God's truth, refused to use any form of spiritual or physical violence to persuade others of the rectitude of his truth. He lived the truth and died witnessing to it.

Shortly after the Women's Multifaith Coalition service, I had a dream. I was lying with my body stretched across a narrow but deep and dark ravine. At the bottom of the sheer cliffs beneath me, a fast current of water foamed across jagged rocks. My feet touched one side of the gap and my hands clutched the other, in such a way that my body formed a bridge between the two sides of the cliffs. Two vast, flat plains stretched behind and in front of me, on both sides of the ravine. I could hear the sounds of guns and screaming behind me, and the land was shrouded in smoke. But the other side was quiet and peaceful: the sun was shining and the sky was clear. Out of the smoke behind me emerged women clasping small children in their arms or dragging children at their sides. I realized that they would have to walk across my back to escape to the other side. I knew that once across, they would find safety.

I have learned to be attentive to the sacred messages carried in dreams. This one conveyed to me that my role was to lay down my life in order to be a bridge towards a different future. I have a foot in both spiritual camps — past and present —

and can provide a way to mediate between the two and to cross from one side to the other, even though I may not live to witness that future.

Those who have attained spiritual maturity are called to be bridges to the future. To resist the temptation to retreat into an imaginary universe of absolute certainties, to overcome our fear of the future with renewed trust in the guidance of God: this is our responsibility to future generations. The revival of interest in the role of Mary Magdalene is part of an expanding, inclusive vision of God. By reclaiming Mary Magdalene's true legacy, we are recognizing the sacredness of sexuality and the spiritual leadership of women. This Magdalene moment calls for women and men, regardless of ethnic background or sexual orientation, to work in mutual partnership to liberate God from the shackles of small-minded sectarianism, so that the life force of God at the heart of all creation will flow through all of us. Thus empowered, we can embrace the difficult and dangerous work of finding a common ground of compassion to unite all religions, and set out to confront the urgent tasks of social and environmental justice. Daniel dances at the edge of our imagination, inviting us to embrace this Magdalene moment and step over the threshold into a more just world. The task awaits, and beckons us onward.

NOTES

ALL BIBLICAL QUOTATIONS are taken from the second edition of *The Good News Bible* in Today's English Version, which was published in 1990. It contains the complete text of the Bible, including the Deuterocanonical and Apocryphal books, and received the *imprimatur*, or seal of approval, of the Most Reverend John F. Wheaton, Archbishop of Hartford, Connecticut. *The Good News Bible* was used in Catholic schools in Toronto when I was teaching theology, and I have continued to use it because I find the translation clear and the language close to modern idiomatic usage.

Prologue

1   In *Our Passion for Justice*, Carter Heyward writes that the struggle for justice is fuelled by the passion of erotic love. "Our eroticism is our desire to participate in making love, making justice in the world: our drive towards one another ... Sexuality is expressed not only between lovers but also in the work of an artist who loves her painting or her poetry, a father

who loves his children, a revolutionary who loves her people."
Heyward continues: "A person of passion, a lover of humanity,
is she or he who enters seriously and intentionally into the
depths of human experience, insists upon its value, and finds
God 'In the exchange of glances heavy with existence' [quoted
from Elie Wiesel]." Carter Heyward, *Our Passion for Justice:
Images of Power, Sexuality, and Liberation* (Cleveland: Pilgrim
Press, 1984), 87.

2   Micah 6:8.

Chapter 1

1   *The Resurrection of Mary Magdalene* chronicles the suppression
of Mary Magdalene's crucial role in the early Christian community and the distortion of her image into that of a repentant
prostitute, using Virginia Woolf in an imaginary conversation.
"I am using Woolf for a project I don't think she would have
scorned though she might have hooted with laughter at it," she
writes. "Her puzzled ruminations about the body, her interest
in the strategies of domination make her a good guide and
companion for this particular project, thinking back through
the Magdalene." Jane Schaberg, *The Resurrection of Mary
Magdalene: Legends, Apocrypha and the Christian Testament*
(New York: Continuum, 2002), 45.

2   Schaberg, *The Resurrection of Mary Magdalene*, 303.

3   Robert J. Miller, ed., *The Complete Gospels: Annotated Scholars
Version* (San Francisco: HarperSanFrancisco, 1994), 363.

4   Miller, *The Complete Gospels*, 365.

5   Miller, *The Complete Gospels*, 365.

6   Antti Marjanen, "Mary Magdalene, A Beloved Disciple,"
in Deirdre Good, ed., *Mariam, the Magdalen and the Mother*

(Bloomington: Indiana University Press, 2005), 57. According to Marjanen, Mary Magdalene should be acknowledged as a founder and leader of the Christian community on a par with the disciple John, often referred to as "the beloved disciple." "As a receiver of special divine revelation and as a spokesperson of a subdued group, namely women, Mary Magdalene of the Gospel of Mary joins in a long-standing prophetic tradition. And as a favourite disciple of Jesus she assumes the role of an apostle, along with the others who have mediated the message of the risen Lord" (58).

7 Ann G. Brock, *Mary Magdalene, the First Apostle: The Struggle for Authority* (Cambridge, MA: Harvard Divinity School, 2003), 78.

8 Brock, *Mary Magdalene, the First Apostle*, 78.

9 The first five books of the Bible, known as the Pentateuch, contain four different traditions known as J (Yahwist), E (Elohist), P (Priestly) and D (Deuteronomist). In Genesis there are two different accounts of the creation of the world. It is clear that the story of Adam and Eve in Chapters 2 and 3 comes from the Yahwist tradition, characterized by the use of the word Yahweh for God and anthropomorphic images of God. The creation story in Chapter 1 comes from the Priestly tradition, a later compilation that dates from roughly 500–300 BCE, the time after the Israelites returned from exile in Babylon. This tradition reflects a more transcendent notion of God.

10 Brock, *Mary Magdalene, the First Apostle*, 13.

11 Hippolytus, *De Cantico*, 24–26, as quoted in Brock, *Mary Magdalene, the First Apostle*, 2. Brock adds, "This reference to female apostles from a third-century Bishop of Rome indicates that at least in some early Christian circles the definition of apostle included both genders."

12 Brock, *Mary Magdalene, the First Apostle*, 131. Brock states: "My research concurs with Robert Murray, who finds that in the

Syriac tradition, those texts that conflate the figure of Mary the Mother with Mary Magdalene appear to be achieving a deliberate and systematic 'superimposition' of the Marys."

13 Brock, *Mary Magdalene, the First Apostle*, 89. The phrase does not necessarily imply a sexual relationship between Jesus and Mary Magdalene. In Gnostic literature, the exchange of a kiss is also used as a metaphor for the transmission of special spiritual power, or as a metaphor for spiritual nourishment.

14 Luke 7:36–50.

15 John 12:1–11.

16 Associated Press report, March 18, 2005, in the *St. Petersburg Times*. www.sptimes.com/2005/03/18/worldandnation/cardinal_tackling__da.shtml.

17 Patricia Beattie Jung, Mary Hunt and Radhika Balakrishnan, eds. *Good Sex: Feminist Perspectives from the World's Religions* (New Brunswick, NJ: Rutgers University Press, 2000), 158. Hunt suggests that in a feminist perspective, sexuality should feature in the broader conversation about human rights. Global interreligious dialogue should recognize and value women's sexuality. Too often, especially in Catholic theology, women's sexuality has been "dangerously domesticated" (161).

18 Brian Swimme and Thomas Berry, *The Universe Story: From the Primordial Flaring Forth to the Ecozoic Era: A Celebration of the Unfolding of the Cosmos* (San Francisco: HarperSanFrancisco, 1994), 73. Berry and Swimme have made the complex deductions of the new cosmology, physics and biology accessible to a wide audience of those in search of an understanding of humanity's place in the universe.

19 Jacques Dupuis, SJ, *Toward a Christian Theology of Religious Pluralism* (Maryknoll, NY: Orbis Books, 1997), 388.

20 Sidney Liebes, Elisabet Sahtouris and Brian Swimme, *A Walk Through Time: From Stardust to Us* (New York: Wiley, 1998), 14.

"Matter responds to its own mutual attraction and begins to follow new ways of allurement ... the universe has a bias for complexity ... [but] each new level of complexity in the universe is accompanied by a new level of vulnerability" (15).

21 Wisdom 8.

22 Elisabeth Schüssler Fiorenza, *Searching the Scriptures*, volume 2: *A Feminist Commentary* (New York: Crossroad, 1994), 21. In the Book of Wisdom, Sophia is given attributes similar to those of Egyptian and Greek divinities. Her partnership with God is described in erotic terms, but she is also honoured for her knowledge, teaching, counsel and justice.

23 From Hafiz, "We Have Not Come to Take Prisoners," in *The Gift: Poems by Hafiz, the Great Sufi Master*, trans. Daniel Ladinsky (New York: Penguin Compass, 1999), 28. Printed with permission.

Chapter 2

1 Matthew 18:6.

2 Exodus 16:14.

3 I Timothy 2:15. This text is now recognized as coming from a later source than the Apostle Paul.

4 Julian of Norwich, *Revelations of Divine Love*, trans. into modern English and with an introduction by Clifton Wolters (Harmondsworth: Penguin, 1966), 171.

5 Julian of Norwich, *Revelations of Divine Love*, 165. Even when writing specifically about Jesus, as opposed to God or the Holy Trinity, Julian freely interchanges female and male genders: "... our patient mother, Jesus, does not want us to run away. Nothing would be more displeasing to him" (178).

6 Jane Schaberg, *The Resurrection of Mary Magdalene*, 103.

7 Susannah Heschel, "Jesus as a Theological Transvestite" in

M. Peskowitz and L. Levitt, eds., *Judaism Since Gender* (New York: Routledge, 1997), 191. Heschel, who is the Eli Black Associate Professor of Jewish Studies at Dartmouth College, has written extensively on the issue of whether Jesus is a Jew or a Christian. Every generation creates an image of Jesus to fit the contemporary political and social context. Heschel's particular area of interest is Christian theology in Nazi Germany, where, she says, Jesus became an Aryan. She contends that Jesus is a boundary figure, who moves in and out of both Jewish and Christian worlds.

8   Luke 7:31–35.

9   Galatians 3:26–28.

10 Marcella Althaus-Reid, *Indecent Theology: Theological Perversions in Sex, Gender and Politics* (London and New York: Routledge, 2000), 23. Argentine feminist theologian Marcella Althaus-Reid contends that the Catholic Church's teachings on the procreative virginity of Mary, Mother of Jesus, have been responsible for the absence of references to healthy female sexual desire in theological teaching. She also points out that, for poor women, the preservation of virginity is an impossible ideal: "Poor women are seldom virgins because poverty in Latin America means crowded conditions of violence and promiscuity, where girls get raped before puberty … women thus get pregnant before they know what their own sexuality is and before they can discover the divinity of lust in their lives" (29).

11 Elisabeth Schüssler Fiorenza, *Jesus: Miriam's Child, Sophia's Prophet* (New York: Continuum, 1994), 165. In a chapter entitled "Was Jesus a Feminist?" in Cullen Murphy's *The Word According to Eve: Women and the Bible in Ancient Times and Our Own* (Boston: Houghton Mifflin, 1998), Schüssler Fiorenza tells the author about the treatment she initially received as one of the first "smart girls" to study theology. She was denied

a scholarship to pursue doctoral work, because, as her professor told her, "As a woman, you have no future possibilities for becoming a professor of theology" (132). Later, when she asked a "distinguished professor" in a theology department in Germany if there were any women in the faculty, his reply seemed to imply that one might just as soon contemplate hiring a talking dog. He turned to his housekeeper and asked sarcastically, "Do you want to be my successor?" (133).

12 Matthew 2:13–15.

13 From Hafiz, "A Crystal Rim," in *The Gift: Poems by Hafiz, the Great Sufi Master*, trans. Daniel Ladinsky (New York: Penguin Compass, 1999), 49. Printed with permission.

Chapter 3

1 Pierre Teilhard de Chardin, SJ, "The Mass on the World," in *Hymn of the Universe*, trans. Gerard Vann (London: Collins, 1970), 29.

2 A priest and scientist whose writings conveyed a spirituality that was far ahead of his time, Teilhard was one of the first thinkers to see that modern science and mysticism are handmaids of each other. Elsewhere, he wrote: "This is what I have learned from my contact with the earth — the diaphany of the divine at the heart of a glowing universe, the divine radiating from the heart of matter aflame." Teilhard de Chardin, SJ, *The Divine Milieu: An Essay on the Interior Life*, trans. with an Introduction by Pierre Leroy, SJ, (London: Collins, 1960), 13.

3 Teilhard de Chardin, "Hymn to Matter," in *Hymn of the Universe*, 65. Teilhard's concept of a universe alive and penetrated by divine energy was revolutionary for the spirituality of his time. "I bless and acclaim you, matter: not as the moralizing preachers depict you, debased, disfigured, a mass of brute forces and base appetites, but as you reveal yourself to me

today in your true nature ... the *divine milieu* charged with creative power" (64).

4   Teilhard de Chardin, *Hymn of the Universe*, 30.

5   Teilhard de Chardin, *Hymn of the Universe*, 23.

6   Teilhard de Chardin, *The Divine Milieu*, 129.

7   Gerard Manley Hopkins, "God's Grandeur," *The New Oxford Book of English Verse*, ed. Helen Gardner (Oxford: Oxford University Press, 1972), 786.

8   "Prologue" from *The Earth Charter*, www.earthcharter.org. In 1987, the United Nations World Commission on Environment and Development issued a call for the creation of a new charter that would set forth fundamental principles for sustainable development, but after the 1992 Rio Earth Summit this was still unfinished business. The Earth Charter was launched in 1994 by Maurice Strong, Secretary General of the Earth Summit, and Mikhail Gorbachev, President of Green Cross International, with support from the Dutch government. An Earth Charter Secretariat was established in Costa Rica. The final version of the Earth Charter was approved at UNESCO headquarters in Paris in 2000. The Four Principles of the Charter are: Respect and Care for the Community of Life; Ecological Integrity; Social and Economic Justice; and Democracy, Non-Violence and Peace.

9   John Shelby Spong, *The Sins of Scripture: Exposing the Bible's Texts of Hate to Reveal the God of Love* (San Francisco: HarperSanFrancisco, 2005), 56. Spong is referring to the work of environmental scientist Lynn White. In "The Historical Roots of our Ecological Crises," an essay published in *Science* 155 (1967), White wrote: "Christianity is the most anthropocentric religion in the world," because it had denied the existence of the gods, spirits and demons that inhabit the natural world and therefore rendered nature less sacred. Spong adds:

"Maybe that is part of the reason why it has taken so long for a global consciousness to develop in the world and why, when that consciousness did emerge, it came from sources outside the Christian religion and was actually in conflict with western views" (56).

10 Diarmuid Ó Murchú, *Evolutionary Faith: Rediscovering God in Our Great Story* (New York: Orbis Books, 2002), 45. According to Ó Murchú, "A fecund emptiness predates the Big Bang. Mystics and sages ... long have suggested an origin to the universe that requires a more mystical and poetic rendition ... In the beginning was silence, a restless stillness, pregnant with potency and meaning, as the Creative Spirit brooded over the void, the quantum vacuum, receptive and waiting to explode into expression and form ... everything that comes into being is under the in-spirited power of the creative life force ... Under the quantum principle, everything is in a state of uncertainty, so even the Nothing became unstable and tiny particles of Something began to form" (44).

11 *Globe and Mail*, April 13, 2005.

12 George Coyne, "God's Chance Creation," *The Tablet*, August 6, 2005, 5. Coyne gave this talk at the Vatican to rebut the assertion by Cardinal Christoph Schönborn of Vienna in an article published in the *New York Times* of July 7, 2005, that belief in evolution is incompatible with the belief in traditional Christian teachings on God's purpose and design in creation. This despite the declaration by the Vatican's Pontifical Academy of Sciences in 1996 that evolution is the most reasonable scientific explanation for the process of the origin and development of life.

13 Diarmuid Ó Murchú, *Quantum Theology: Spiritual Implications of the New Physics*, rev. ed. (New York: Crossroad, 2004), 220.

14 I am using the story of the creation and fall of humanity as an

illustration of a spiritual, not a literal, truth. The mythology of these two chapters of Genesis serves as an attempt to explain the existence of evil.

15 John 20:17.

16 Diarmuid Ó Murchú, *Religion in Exile: A Spiritual Homecoming* (New York: Crossroad, 2000), 160.

17 Rosemary Radford Ruether, *Integrating Ecofeminism, Globalization, and World Religions* (Lanham, MD: Rowman & Littlefield, 2005), 125. Ecofeminism, according to Ruether, views nature as a living matrix of interconnection that provides a basis for an alternative vision and structure for all relationships. In addition to rejecting the separation of the divine from the earth, Ruether critiques the use of the divine to reinforce gender stereotypes or the dominance of the human over the natural world.

18 Quoted in James Conlon, *At the Edge of Our Longing: Unspoken Hunger for Sacredness and Depth* (Ottawa: Novalis, 2004), 178.

19 Matthew 25:40.

20 For Dorothy Stang, see Christl Dabu, "Dorothy Stang: Defender of the Amazon Rain Forest," *Catholic New Times*, May 8, 2004, 14. According to an article published in *The Independent* on December 9, 2005, the two men accused of shooting Stang, Rayfran Sales and Clodoaido Batista, are part of a widespread conspiracy of wealthy loggers and ranchers who are the real villains in the destruction of the rainforest.

21 Jane Jacobs, *Dark Age Ahead* (Toronto: Random House, 2004), 171. Jacobs asks the question: how can a culture avoid falling into a Dark Age? If we recognize the signs of decline and act upon them, we may be able to save ourselves from following the same fate as the Roman Empire. In the United States especially, the current fortress and fundamentalist mentality, which is founded on self-deception and hubris, must be countered by a return to original values of true democracy and accountability.

22 Jacobs, *Dark Age Ahead*, 24.

23 Jared Diamond, *Collapse: How Societies Choose to Fail or Succeed* (New York: Viking, 2004), 487–96.

24 Wangari Maathai, Nobel Peace Prize Acceptance Speech, December 10, 2004. See Green Belt Movement: www.green-beltmovement.org. In an interview with Mia Macdonald, published on www.beliefnet.com on 16 April 2005, Maathai links her environmental activism with her Christian roots. She suggests that on Easter Monday, Christians all over the world could plant trees in celebration of the regeneration of the whole of creation symbolized by Christ's resurrection from death on the tree of Calvary.

25 Kabir, "What Kind of God?," in *Love Poems from God: Twelve Sacred Voices from the East and West*, trans. Daniel Ladinsky (New York: Penguin Compass, 2002), 213. Printed with permission.

Chapter 4

1 Stephen Lewis, the United Nations Secretary General's special envoy for HIV/AIDS in Africa, called his 2005 Massey Lectures on the AIDS epidemic in Africa, *Race Against Time*. "The pandemic of HIV/AIDS feels as though it will go on forever ... No one is untouched. Virtually every country in east and southern Africa is a nation of mourners." Stephen Lewis, *Race Against Time* (Toronto: Anansi, 2005), 1–2.

2 For more on the connection between the plight of African women and the AIDS crisis, see Lewis, *Race Against Time*, Chapter 4: "Women: Half the World, Barely Represented." On page 143, Lewis points out that the African countries that score lowest on the UN's gender development index all have a high prevalence of HIV infection.

3   Isabel Apawo Phiri, "African Women of Faith Speak Out in an HIV/AIDS Era," in *African Women, HIV/AIDS and Faith Communities* (Pietermaritzburg, South Africa: Cluster Publications, 2003), 15.

4   Lewis, *Race Against Time*, 55.

5   KAIROS, *Canadian Ecumenical Justice Initiatives: Safe Third Country Agreement* (Toronto: United Church of Canada, 2004), 1.

6   Luke 8:1–3.

7   Acts 2:44–45.

8   Acts 4:32–35.

9   Acts 5:2.

10   Acts 5:3.

11   Matthew 16:23.

12   Mark 10:17–25.

13   Acts 5:7–10.

14   Acts 5:11.

15   Branko Milanovic, *Worlds Apart: Measuring International and Global Inequality* (Princeton: Princeton University Press, 2005), 2.

16   For information on *MuseLetter*, see www.museletter.com.

17   Richard Heinberg, *Powerdown: Options and Actions for a Post-Carbon World* (Gabriola Island, B.C.: New Society, 2004), 117. According to Heinberg, relying on the development of new energy sources to replace society's dependence on the diminishing supply of fossil fuels is merely wishful thinking. Even the discovery of a perfect energy source could not sustain economic growth indefinitely.

18   Exodus 16:4.

19   Ched Myers, *The Biblical Version of Sabbath Economics* (Washington, DC: Church of the Saviour Press, 2001).

20   Myers, *The Biblical Version of Sabbath Economics*, 14

21   Luke 4:18–19.

22   For more information on the Hundred Mile Diet, see http://thetyee.ca.

23 Heinberg, *Powerdown*, 155–58. Just as the monasteries of the medieval period preserved the classical literature and the Latin language after the fall of the Roman Empire, these communities would conserve knowledge and tools, though the latter would be limited if a worldwide catastrophe destroyed the electrical grid system. These "preservationist communities" would also preserve the social structure of democracy, which could be threatened by the encroachment of what Heinberg calls "survivalist communities," predatory small groups intent only on satisfying individual needs.

24 From Hafiz, "Please," in *The Gift: Poems by Hafiz, the Great Sufi Master*, trans. Daniel Ladinsky (New York: Penguin Compass, 1999), 115. Printed with permission.

Chapter 5

1 Michael Adams, *Fire and Ice: The United States, Canada and the Myth of Converging Values* (Toronto: Viking Canada, 2003), 50. According to Adams, while a greater percentage of Americans appear to be clinging to religion and patriarchal family values, Canadians have distanced themselves from organized religion and traditional family values.

2 Adams, *Fire and Ice*, 147. Adams believes that Canadian and American cultures will remain different, despite increasing economic convergence. On page 126 he states: "In my nightmares, I may see the American fire melting the Canadian ice and then dream of the waters created by the melting ice drowning the fire, but this will not happen ... the two cultures will continue side by side, converging their economies, technologies and now their security and defence policies, but will continue to diverge in the ways that most people in

each country, I believe, will continue to celebrate."

3   Jennifer Welsh, *At Home in the World: Canada's Global Vision for the Twenty-First Century* (Toronto: HarperCollins, 2004), 189. According to Welsh, Canada's model citizenship is characterized by liberal democracy, pluralism, bilingualism and its refugee and immigration policy, together with a strong culture of human rights and an internationalist outlook in foreign policy.

4   Richard Florida, *The Rise of the Creative Class: And How It's Transforming Work, Leisure, Community and Everyday Life* (New York: Basic Books, 2002). Florida outlines a measure of economic growth called the Creativity Index. Diversity, of which openness to gays and lesbians is a key measure, is one of the six measurements for a city's ranking on the list. A city's success will depend on its ability to attract the "super-creative core class" of scientists, engineers, architects, professors, writers, artists, and entertainers.

5   Welsh, *At Home in the World*, 164.

6   *The Canadian Charter of Rights and Freedoms*, Section 27: "This Charter shall be interpreted in a manner consistent with the preservation and enhancement of the multicultural heritage of Canadians." Section 28: "Notwithstanding anything in this Charter, the rights and freedoms referred to in it are guaranteed equally to male and female persons."

7   Boyd's 150-page review, *Dispute Resolution in Family Law: Protecting Choice, Promoting Inclusion* (Ministry of the Attorney General, Province of Ontario, December 2004), was divided into eight sections concerned with arbitration in family and inheritance law. She recommended that arbitration using religious principles should be allowed in family law and that Muslim principles should be included as long as they do not violate Canadian law.

8   Ingrid Peritz, "Shirin Ebadi Decries Islamic Law for Canada," *Globe and Mail*, June 14, 2005, A7.

9   Jane Schaberg, *The Resurrection of Mary Magdalene: Legends, Apocrypha and the Christian Testament* (New York: Continuum, 2002), 40. On page 21, Schaberg calls Woolf her "intellectual companion for this study of the Magdalene," because, even though Woolf was raised as an atheist, her work is replete with religious and spiritual questions and allusions.

10 Koran 5:14. Quoted in Diana Eck, *Encountering God: A Spiritual Journey from Bozeman to Benares* (Boston: Beacon Press, 2003), 189.

11 Thomas Aquinas, *Summa Theologica*, Part 1, Question 47. Quoted in Anne Lonergan, *Thomas Berry and the New Cosmology* (New London, CT: Twenty-Third Publications, 1987), 30.

12 Bartolome de las Casas (1474–1566) travelled with the conquistador Gonzalo Fernandez de Oviedo to Hispaniola in 1502. Shocked by the treatment meted out to the slaves and indigenous peoples in the name of Christianity, he devoted the rest of his life to raising awareness of the human rights of conquered peoples. His three-volume *History of the Indies* is considered the forerunner of modern liberation theology. He travelled to Mexico, Nicaragua, Peru and Guatemala and eventually back to the court of Charles v of Spain in pursuit of better legal protection for the indigenous peoples of South America.

13 James Fowler, *Faithful Change: The Personal and Public Challenge of Postmodern Life* (Nashville, TN: Abingdon Press, 1996).

14 Julian of Norwich, *Revelations of Divine Love*, trans. into modern English and with an introduction by Clifton Wolters (Harmondsworth: Penguin, 1966), 165.

15 Miroslav Volf, *Exclusion and Embrace: A Theological Exploration of Identity, Otherness and Reconciliation* (Nashville, TN: Abingdon Press, 1996), 182. According to Volf, in a Christianity modelled on the Trinity there can be no fixed essence of femininity and masculinity but rather an interchange of mutual relationships within a diversity of cultural settings.

16 Mark 8:1–10.

17 Genesis 3:8.

18 Ecumenical Consultation, Baar, Switzerland, January 1990. As quoted in Jacques Dupuis, sj, *Toward a Christian Theology of Religious Pluralism* (Maryknoll, NY: Orbis Books, 1997), 200.

19 Thirteenth Annual Meeting of the Indian Theological Association, December 28–31, 1989. Dupuis, *Towards a Christian Theology of Religious Pluralism*, 199.

20 Riane Eisler, *Sacred Pleasure: Sex, Myth and the Politics of the Body — New Paths to Power and Love* (San Francisco: Harper SanFrancisco, 1995). In the final chapter, "The New Adams and the New Eves," Eisler states that there is no guarantee that we will succeed in freeing ourselves from the myths that still bind us to dysfunctional, unjust and painful ways of living and dying. "In Christian tradition we have many of Jesus' teachings of stereotypically feminine values such as compassion and non-violence ... while others are going outside this tradition in search of the myths, images and rites we need for a more peaceful and equitable world ... a reinvestment of our bodies and our intimate relations with the sacred is one of the most important building blocks for a new partnership spirituality that is both immanent and transcendent" (380).

21 Quoted in Diana Eck, *Encountering God*, 200.

22 From Hafiz, "I Have Come Into the World to See This," in *Love Poems from God: Twelve Sacred Voices from the East and West*, trans. Daniel Ladinsky (New York: Penguin Compass, 2002), 159. Printed with permission.

SELECTED REFERENCES

Abou El Naga, Shereen. "New Politics, Old Identities: Arab Women in (Their) English Words." *Agenda/Feminist Media* 54 (2002): 60–73.

Adams, Michael. *Fire and Ice: The United States, Canada and the Myth of Converging Values.* Toronto: Viking Canada, 2003.

Alliaume, Karen Trimble. "The Risks of Repeating Ourselves: Reading Feminist/Womanist Figures of Jesus." *Cross Currents* 48/2 (Summer 1998): 198ff. Also available online at www.crosscurrents.org//alliaume.htm.

Althaus-Reid, Marcella. *Indecent Theology: Theological Perversions in Sex, Gender and Politics.* London and New York: Routledge, 2000.

Armstrong, Karen. *A History of God: The 4,000-Year Quest of Judaism, Christianity and Islam.* New York: Knopf, 1993.

——— . *The Spiral Staircase: My Climb Out of Darkness.* New York: Knopf, 2004.

Barlow, Maude. *Too Close for Comfort: Canada's Future Within Fortress North America.* Toronto: McClelland & Stewart, 2005.

Bauckham, Richard. *Gospel Women: Studies of the Named Women in the Gospels.* Grand Rapids, MI: Eerdmans, 2002.

Birx, James H. "The Phenomenon of Pierre Teilhard de Chardin." Given at the Harbinger symposium *Religion and Science: The Best of Enemies — The Worst of Friends*, May 4, 1997. Available online at www.theharbinger.org/articles/rel_sci/birx.

Boyd, Marion. *Dispute Resolution in Family Law: Protecting Choice, Promoting Inclusion*. Toronto: Ministry of the Attorney General, Province of Ontario, December 2004.

Braybrooke, Marcus. *Faith and Interfaith in a Global Age*. London: CoNexus Press, 1998.

Brock, Ann G. *Mary Magdalene, the First Apostle: The Struggle for Authority*. Cambridge, MA: Harvard Divinity School, 2003.

Brown, Dan. *The Da Vinci Code*. New York: Doubleday, 2003.

Burstein, Dan, ed. *Secrets of the Code: The Unauthorized Guide to the Mysteries Behind the Da Vinci Code*. New York: CDS Books, 2004.

Calamai, Peter. "The Dark Side of the Universe." *Toronto Star*, October 23, 2005, D4.

Carr, Geoffrey. "The Proper Study of Mankind." *The Economist*, December 24, 2005, 3–12.

Chilton, Bruce. *Mary Magdalene: A Biography*. New York: Doubleday, 2005.

——— . *Rabbi Jesus: An Intimate Biography*. New York: Doubleday, 2000.

Christ, Carol. *She Who Changes: Re-Imagining the Divine in the World*. New York: Palgrave Macmillan, 2003.

Claiborne, Shane. *The Irresistible Revolution: Living as an Ordinary Radical*. Grand Rapids, MI: Zondervan, 2006.

Cleary, William. *Prayers to an Evolutionary God*. Woodstock, VT: Skylight Paths, 2004.

Conlon, James. *At the Edge of Our Longing: Unspoken Hunger for Sacredness and Depth*. Ottawa: Novalis, 2004.

Conway, Janet M. *Identity, Place, Knowledge: Social Movements Contesting Globalization*. Halifax: Fernwood Publishing, 2004.

Coyne, George. "God's Chance Creation." *The Tablet*, August 6, 2005, 5–6.

———. "Infinite Wonder of the Divine." *The Tablet*, December 10, 2005, 7–8.

Crossan, John D. *Jesus: A Revolutionary Biography*. New York: HarperSanFrancisco, 1994.

Diamond, Jared. *Collapse: How Societies Choose to Fail or Succeed*. New York: Viking, 2004.

Dunsky, Dan. "The Anti-Nation." *Toronto Star*, January 8, 2006, D.

Dupuis, Jacques, SJ. "Jesus with an Asian Face." 1999. Available online at www.sedos.org/english/dupuis_1.htm.

———. "Religious Pluralism and the Christological Debate." 2001. Available online at www.sedos.org/english/dupuis.htm.

———. *Toward a Christian Theology of Religious Pluralism*. Maryknoll, NY: Orbis Books, 1997.

Eck, Diana. *Encountering God: A Spiritual Journey from Bozeman to Benares*. Boston: Beacon Press, 1993; reprinted, 2003.

Eisler, Riane. *The Chalice and the Blade*. Cambridge, MA: Harper & Row, 1987.

———. *Sacred Pleasure: Sex, Myth and the Politics of the Body — New Paths to Power and Love*. San Francisco: HarperSanFrancisco, 1995.

Ellison, Marvin M. "Sexual Ethics without the F Word: No to Sexual Fundamentalism, Yes to an Ethical Eroticism." Jack Reynolds Lecture. Toronto School of Theology, February 26, 2003.

Flannery, Tim. *The Weather Makers: How Man Is Changing the Climate and What It Means for Life on Earth*. New York: Atlantic Monthly Press, 2006.

Florida, Richard. "Creative Class War: How the GOP's Anti-Elitism Could Ruin America's Economy." *Washington Monthly* (Jan/Feb 2004). Available online at www.washingtonmonthly.com/features/2004/0401.florida.html.

————. "The Greatest Political Threat of Our Time." *The Globalist* (March 2003). Available online at www.theglobalist.com/DBWeb/printStoryId.aspx?StoryId=4719.

————. *The Rise of the Creative Class: And How It's Transforming Work, Leisure, Community and Everyday Life*. New York: Basic Books, 2002. Available online at www.washingtonmonthly.com/features/2001/0205.florida.html.

Fowler, James. *Faithful Change: The Personal and Public Challenges of Postmodern Life*. Nashville, TN: Abingdon Press, 1996.

Fox, Matthew. *One River Many Wells: Wisdom Springing from Global Faiths*. New York: Tarcher, 2000.

Fulkerson, Mary M. "Neither Male Nor Female: Church Debates and the Politics of Identity." *The Witness* (April 2000). Available online at www.thewitness.org/archive/april2000/neithermalenor.html.

Gastle, Chuck. "Defining Canada's Role." *Toronto Star*, November 8, 2004, A.

George, Margaret. *Mary, Called Magdalene*. New York: Viking, 2002.

Good, Deirdre, ed. *Mariam, the Magdalen, and the Mother*. Bloomington: Indiana University Press, 2005.

Gornik, Mark R. *To Live in Peace: Biblical Faith and the Changing City*. Grand Rapids, MI: Eerdmans, 2002.

Grim, John and Mary. *Teilhard de Chardin: A Short Biography*. Teilhard Studies No. 11. Chambersburg, PA: American Teilhard Association for the Future of Man and ANIMA, 1984.

Hafiz. *The Gift: Poems by Hafiz, the Great Sufi Master*. Trans. Daniel Ladinsky. New York: Penguin Compass, 1999.

Haight, Roger, SJ. *Jesus, Symbol of God*. Maryknoll, NY: Orbis Books, 1999.

Hallman, David C., ed. *Ecotheology: Voices from South and North*. Maryknoll, NY: Orbis Books, 1994.

————. *A Place in Creation: Ecological Visions in Science, Religion and Economics*. Toronto: United Church Publishing House, 1992.

Heinberg, Richard. *Powerdown: Options and Actions for a Post-Carbon World*. Gabriola Island, B.C.: New Society, 2004.

Heschel, Susannah. "Jesus as a Theological Transvestite." In M. Peskowitz and L. Levitt, eds., *Judaism Since Gender*. New York: Routledge, 1997.

Heyward, Carter. *Our Passion for Justice: Images of Power, Sexuality, and Liberation*. New York: Pilgrim Press, 1984.

———. *Saving Jesus from Those Who Are Right: Rethinking What It Means to Be Christian*. Minneapolis: Fortress Press, 1999.

———. *Touching Our Strength: The Erotic as Power and the Love of God*. San Francisco: Harper & Row, 1989.

Hughes, Robert Davis. "Christian Theology of Interfaith Dialogue: Defining the Emerging Fourth Option." *Sewanee Theological Revue* 40 (1997): 383–408.

Jacobs, Jane. *Dark Age Ahead*. Toronto: Random House, 2004.

Julian of Norwich. *Revelations of Divine Love*. Trans. into modern English and with an introduction by Clifton Wolters. Harmondsworth: Penguin, 1966.

Jung, Patricia Beattie, Mary Hunt and Radhika Balakrishnan, eds. *Good Sex: Feminist Perspectives from the World's Religions*. New Brunswick, NJ: Rutgers University Press, 2000.

KAIROS (Canadian Ecumenical Justice Initiatives). "Safe Third Country Agreement," December 17, 2004. Available online at www.kairoscanada.org/e/refugees/SafeCountry.

Knitter, Paul. *One Earth, Many Religions: Multifaith Dialogue and Global Responsibility*. Maryknoll, NY: Orbis Books, 1995.

———. *Jesus and the Other Names: Christian Mission and Global Responsibility*. Maryknoll, NY: Orbis Books, 1996.

Ladinsky, Daniel, trans. *Love Poems from God: Twelve Sacred Voices from the East and West*. New York: Penguin Compass, 2002.

Leloup, Jean-Yves and Jacob Needleman (Foreword). *The Gospel of Mary Magdalene*. Rochester, VT: Inner Traditions, 2002.

Lewis, Stephen. *Race Against Time*. Toronto: Anansi, 2005.

Liebes, Sidney, Elisabet Sahtouris and Brian Swimme. *A Walk Through Time: From Stardust to Us*. New York: Wiley, 1998.

Lonergan et al. *Thomas Berry and the New Cosmology*. New London, CT: Twenty-Third Publications, 1987.

Maathai, Wangari. Nobel Peace Prize Acceptance Speech, December 10, 2004. Available online at http://gbmna.org/a.php?id=34.

Masson, Robert. "Karl Rahner: A Brief Biography." Available online at the Karl Rahner Society website, www.krs.stjohnsem.edu/karlrahner.htm.

McLachlin, The Rt. Hon B. "The Civilization of Difference." Fourth Annual Lafontaine-Baldwin Lecture, 2003. Available online at www.oper-ation-dialogue.com/lafontaine-baldwin/e/2003_speech_1.html.

Milanovic, Branko. *Worlds Apart: Measuring International and Global Inequality*. Princeton: Princeton University Press, 2005.

Miller, Robert J., ed. *The Complete Gospels: Annotated Scholars Version*. San Francisco: HarperSanFrancisco, 1994.

Murphy, Cullen. *The Word According to Eve: Women and the Bible in Ancient Times and Our Own*. Boston: Houghton Mifflin, 1998.

Myers, Ched. *The Biblical Vision of Sabbath Economics*. Washington, DC: Church of the Saviour Press, 2001.

Myers et al. *Say to This Mountain: Mark's Story of Discipleship*. Maryknoll, NY: Orbis Books, 1996.

Nyeck, Sybille Ngo. "Faith and Dogma in a Cultural Third World." April 2004. Available online at www.thewitness.org/agw/nyeckenglish040204.html.

Ó Murchú, Diarmuid. *Evolutionary Faith: Rediscovering God in Our Great Story*. Maryknoll, NY: Orbis Books, 2002.

———. *Quantum Theology: Spiritual Implications of the New Physics*. Rev. ed. New York: Crossroad, 2004.

———. *Religion in Exile: A Spiritual Homecoming*. New York: Crossroad, 2000.

Pagels, Elaine. *The Gnostic Gospels.* New York: Random House, 1979.

Pettifor, Anne. "The Urgent Need for Economic Transformation: Subordinating the Interests of Finance Capital to Human Rights." Available online at www.jubileeresearch.org/analysis/articles/economic_transformationann.htm.

Phiri, Isabel Apawo, ed. *African Women, HIV/AIDS, and Faith Communities.* Pietermaritzburg, South Africa: Cluster Publications, 2003.

Pieris, Aloysius, SJ. *An Asian Theology of Liberation.* Maryknoll, NY: Orbis Books, 1988.

———. *God's Reign for God's Poor: A Return to the Jesus Formula.* Colombo, Sri Lanka: Ecumenical Institute for Study And Dialogue, 1999.

Rakoczy, Susan, IHM. *In Her Name: Women Doing Theology.* Pietermaritzburg, South Africa: Cluster Publications, 2004.

Ruether, Rosemary Radford. *Goddesses and the Divine Feminine: A Western Religious History.* Berkeley: University of California Press, 2005.

———. *Integrating Ecofeminism, Globalization, and World Religions.* Lanham, MD: Rowman & Littlefield, 2005.

———. *Sexism and God-Talk: Toward a Feminist Theology.* Boston: Beacon Press, 1983.

Schaberg, Jane. *The Resurrection of Mary Magdalene: Legends, Apocrypha and the Christian Testament.* New York: Continuum, 2002.

Schüssler Fiorenza, Elisabeth. *Jesus: Miriam's Child, Sophia's Prophet.* New York: Continuum, 1994.

———. *Searching the Scriptures,* 2 vols. Vol. 1: *A Feminist Introduction;* vol. 2: *A Feminist Commentary.* New York: Crossroad, 1993–94.

Schut, Michael, ed. *Simpler Living, Compassionate Life: A Christian Perspective.* Denver: Living the Good News, 1999.

Seife, Charles. *Alpha and Omega: The Search for the Beginning and End of the Universe.* New York: Viking, 2003.

Smith, Alisa. "Living on the Hundred Mile Diet." Available online at http://thetyee.ca//life/2005/06/28/hundredmilediet/.

Spong, John Shelby. *The Sins of Scripture: Exposing the Bible's Texts of Hate to Reveal the God of Love.* San Francisco: Harper SanFrancisco, 2005.

Swimme, Brian, and Thomas Berry. *The Universe Story: From the Primordial Flaring Forth to the Ecozoic Era — A Celebration of the Unfolding of the Cosmos.* San Francisco: HarperSanFrancisco, 1994.

Teilhard de Chardin, Pierre. *Hymn of the Universe.* Trans. Gerald Vann. London: Collins, 1970.

Tucker, Mary E. "Sacred Connections: The Emerging Alliance of World Religions and Equality." *Resurgence* 214 (Sept/Oct 2002). Available online at www.resurgence.org/contents/214.htm.

UNESCO. *The Earth Charter.* The Earth Charter Initiative, March 2000. www.earthcharter.org.

Vaney, Neil. *Christ in a Grain of Sand: An Ecological Journey with the Spiritual Exercises.* Notre Dame, IN: Ave Maria Press, 2004.

Volf, Miroslav. *Exclusion and Embrace: A Theological Exploration of Identity, Otherness and Reconciliation.* Nashville, TN: Abingdon Press, 1996.

Welsh, Jennifer. *At Home in the World: Canada's Global Vision for the 21st Century.* Toronto: HarperCollins, 2004.

Wright, Ronald. *A Short History of Progress.* Toronto: Anansi, 2004.

Wu, Olivia. "Environment in Focus: Diet for a Sustainable Planet." *San Francisco Examiner,* June 1, 2005, 7.

INDEX